Off the Beaten Trail

50 fantastic unknown hikes in NW Oregon and SW Washington

Matt Reeder

ISBN: 978-0-9889125-0-2
First edition, 2013

All photos by Matt Reeder except pages 44, 78 and 142 (Wendy Rodgers).

Maps in this book were created using National Geographic's *Topo!* software with express permission from National Geographic. For more information, go to http://www.nationalgeographic.com

Cover photo: Mount Hood from Owl Point (Hike 28)
Frontispiece photo: White River Falls (Hike 34)
Back photo: Basin Lakes (Hike 14)

Acknowledgements

To Wendy, my partner on and off the trail, without whom I would be lost.

To Ted, my stepfather and first hiking partner, who taught me to appreciate the value of solitude and to never give up. Thanks for making me hike those switchbacks!

To Karl, Keith, Cabe, Chelsea, Sarah, Joe and everyone else who hiked with me and helped me research this book. You've helped me in more ways than you could possibly imagine and you still kept coming back for more. Merci beaucoup, mes amis!

Thanks to all of my friends and family for believing in me. You always make everything better and you stuck with me through the long process of writing this book. You guys are awesome!

To Portland Hikers: I never would have even imagined I could do this without the great people on http://www.portlandhikers.org. You gave me ideas, inspiration, kept me updated on current conditions and made me laugh more times than I could ever count. I will be in debt to all of you for a great long while.

To the Mazamas: Thank you for giving me the opportunity to lead hikes and serve your fine organization. It's an honor for me!

HIKES:

FOREST PARK (PORTLAND)

1. Newton Road Loop
2. St. Johns Bridge Loop

COAST AND COAST RANGE

3. Upper Salmonberry River
4. Lower Salmonberry River
5. Netarts Spit
6. Valley of the Giants
7. Mary's Peak

SOUTHWEST WASHINGTON

8. Silver Star Mountain via Starway
9. Black Hole Falls
10. Goat Marsh Lake
11. Butte Camp
12. Cave and Curly Falls
13. Quartz Creek
14. Indian Racetrack / Red Mtn
15. Lookingglass Lake

COLUMBIA RIVER GORGE

16. Rock of Ages Ridge
17. Wauneka Point
18. Ruckel Ridge
19. Dry Creek Falls via Herman Crk
20. Indian Mountain
21. Bald Butte
22. Stacker Butte
23. Swale Canyon
24. Deschutes River Trail

MOUNT HOOD

25. Horseshoe Ridge
26. Yocum Ridge
27. Bald Mountain via Lolo Pass
28. Owl Point
29. Boulder Lake Loop
30. Fifteenmile Creek
31. Flag Point and West Point
32. Tygh Creek
33. Kinzel Cabin
34. White River Falls

CLACKAMAS RIVER COUNTRY

35. The Other Eagle Creek
36. Fish Creek
37. Fish Creek Mountain
38. Mount Mitchell
39. Thunder Mountain
40. Whetstone Mountain
41. Bull of the Woods
42. Elk Lake Creek

MOUNT JEFFERSON

43. Henline Falls
44. Battle Ax
45. Hawk Mountain
46. Ruddy Hill
47. Bear Point
48. Jefferson Park
49. Wild Cheat / Triangulation Peak
50. Table Lake

INTRODUCTION

"May your trails be crooked, winding, lonesome, dangerous, leading to the most amazing view."
- **Edward Abbey**

Breathtaking mountains, towering old-growth forests, spectacular waterfalls in every shape and form, mile after mile of rugged coastline, sagebrush-scented Ponderosa pine high desert: to live in the Pacific Northwest is to be spoiled with immense natural riches. For those of us who love to hike the possibilities are seemingly endless. Living in such close proximity to the Portland metro area however, can make it difficult to find a sense of solitude and wildness within our surrounding natural areas. The principle of this book is simple: you should not have to sacrifice solitude for scenery. Thankfully, for every crowded, popular trail, there are many other places – wildly spectacular places – that have yet to be discovered by area hikers. With a simple willingness to explore some of the most overlooked places in northwest Oregon and southwest Washington, you can have your cake and eat it too.

The hikes in this book are varied. Hikes are divided into seven regions: Forest Park in Portland, the Coast and Coast Range, Southwest Washington, the Columbia River Gorge, Mount Hood, Clackamas River Country, and the Mount Jefferson areas. Hikes range from short leg-stretchers to multi-day treks, though almost every hike offers additional options to shorten or lengthen your adventure. Many hikes are on well-maintained tread while others are on abandoned trails, and still others are on long-lost forest roads. You will find new routes to familiar places, but you will find many more places you may not have heard of even if you've been hiking for many years in the Portland area. With this book, you will visit places that will wow even the most seasoned hikers you know. Bring a camera!

What makes these hikes "off the beaten trail"?
Hikes in this book were judged subjectively based on scenery, solitude and ease of access. Hikes must be compelling enough to do more than once. In the course of researching this book I hiked hundreds of trails. Some turned out to be far too popular to include in this book while others turned out to be not all that interesting. The hikes in this book were hits in both categories. You will find yourself returning over and over again to these special places. I certainly have not minded hiking them again and again over the years.

The primary geographic qualification is that trailheads be no more than a 2 hour and 30 minute drive from the Portland metropolitan area. This, of course, depends on where you live (if you happen to live in the Portland area at all). Why 2 hours and 30 minutes? I have found that this is the absolute maximum people are willing to drive (one-way) for a day hike. However much you are willing to drive, you should find many new places not far from where you live.

Ease of hikes:
I do not rate hikes by their difficulty. In my experience, the difficulty of a hike is based on so many subjective factors that any rating is completely pointless. Some people find hikes of 5 miles and no elevation gain to be difficult while others can hike as much as 30 miles with 6,000 or more feet of elevation in a single day. Complicating matters further are trail and weather conditions. For example, a hike with little shade and a moderate amount of elevation gain can become a very difficult hike on a hot day. I remember the first time I hiked Elk Lake Creek (Hike 42), the trail had not been maintained in many years and there were hundreds of downed trees on the trail, turning a moderate hike into a very difficult and tiring day. Everything is subjective.

If you simply must have difficulty ratings, here is a good guide:

* **Easy** – less than 7 miles and 1,000 feet of elevation gain
* **Moderate** – 6 – 10 miles with less than 2,000 feet of elevation gain
* **Difficult** – 8 or more miles with more than 2,000 feet of elevation gain
* **Very Difficult** – 12 or more miles with more than 3,000 feet of elevation gain
* **Iron Man** – 15 or more miles with more than 4,000 feet of elevation gain

Road Access:
All of the hikes in this book are accessible with a standard 2-wheel drive low-clearance vehicle. Naturally, some roads are better than others. While many trailheads in this book are found on 2-lane paved roads, others are at the far end of gravel forest roads. I have made every effort to ensure the accuracy of my driving directions and clearly explain the road conditions where there might be a cause for concern. US and state highways are labeled as US or OR (for example: US 26 and OR 214) while forest roads (which are maintained by the Forest Service, are labeled as FR (for example, FR 46 or FR 4690).

While you can expect that paved roads listed in this book will be well-maintained and easy to drive on a yearly basis, the condition of gravel roads tends to change with each year and in some cases every season. Roads that do not receive regular maintenance are the ones most likely to be in rough shape. If you are still not sure about road conditions after reading this book, check with your local ranger station or ask at Portland Hikers (http://www.portlandhikers.org) – somebody there will probably know.

Do **NOT** use your GPS to find road directions once you are out in remote areas –

while they are frequently correct, the times they are not can lead you down roads that are no longer maintained, or in some cases, no longer exist. If you are unsure of directions or become lost, backtrack until you reach a well-traveled road. I also recommend purchasing a National Forest map or printing a general area map from topographic software to help you navigate the occasionally confusing backroads of our National Forests and BLM land.

A note about trail maintenance:
As this is a book about lesser-known trails, you should assume that trail maintenance will be infrequent at best. While some trails, particularly those in the area around Mount Hood and every segment of the Pacific Crest Trail in this book, receive annual maintenance, many other trails, particularly those in the Badger Creek and Bull of the Woods Wilderness Areas, are maintained only once every ten years or so. Some of the Gorge Trails listed in this book, such as Rock of Ages Ridge and Ruckel Ridge, are permanently considered unmaintained. I have made every effort to describe unmaintained trails in great detail, noting every turn and difficult spot. You should be able to follow every trail in this book even in conditions that are less than optimal.

HIKING PREPARATION: A DISCLAIMER
Before we get started, a disclaimer is necessary. Hiking is a joyous, wonderfully fun activity. Without taking proper precautions, it can also be very dangerous. Please be prepared wherever you go, whether it is to Forest Park in Portland or Table Lake in the Mount Jefferson Wilderness.

I have spent countless days on the trail and countless nights on my computer working to ensure the accuracy of every piece of information in this book. This does not mean that your experience will be the same as mine. Trail and road conditions change with every successive season. Wildfires, rainstorms, windstorms, heavy snowpack, avalanches and logging operations can cause great damage to roads and trails. You may find that something I have described is factually inaccurate as a result. If so, I would love to hear about it!

The best line of defense against accidents and unfortunate circumstance is to go into each hike as prepared as possible. Bring a topographic map of each place you go. I have provided a map for most of the hikes in this book but you should still bring an additional map if possible. You should also check online or at your local ranger station to inquire about the most current conditions anywhere you go. This includes snow levels in the mountains during the winter and fire danger in summer. By preparing yourself before each outing, you can avoid becoming one of those people on the news.

The Ten Essentials:
Given that you will be hiking into little-known areas with this book, you should plan on being even more prepared than you would be for an average day hike. This means that you should know exactly where you are going and notifying at least one person of your plans for that day. This also means carrying the Ten Essentials with you at all times. They are:

1. A map of the area (preferably topographic and highly-detailed)
2. Compass and/or GPS
3. Extra food
4. Extra water (especially in the summer)
5. Extra clothing (no cotton!)
6. A headlamp or flashlight
7. First Aid Kit
8. waterproof matches or a reliable lighter
9. Sunglasses and sunscreen
10. Knife and/or multitool with knife

There are five more items I highly recommend bringing to supplement the ten essentials:

11. A Water filter or water purification tablets
12. An extra pair of warm socks wrapped in a waterproof plastic bag
13. Duct tape (useful for repairing tears and emergency waterproofing)
14. A whistle
15. An emergency space blanket

While you should not need to bring your entire life with you on a hike, these fifteen items, most of them lightweight and easy to pack, will save your life in an emergency.

Additional Resources:
These websites will give you a lot of useful additional information as you plan your hikes off the beaten trail.

* **Portland Hikers** (http://www.portlandhikers.org) – An online forum and field guide dedicated to hiking, snowshoeing and backpacking in the Portland area. In the forums you can view trip reports for up-to-date information on hikes all across the region. Stop here before you leave the house for current information and browse the forums for great ideas!

* **Washington Trails Association** (http://www.wta.org) – This fantastic organization maintains trails all across the Evergreen State. Join one of their work parties – they're great fun! The website also features a comprehensive hiking guide with trip reports and directions.

* **Trail Advocates** (http://www.trailadvocate.org) – This is like the WTA but for the Clackamas Ranger District. This group of dedicated volunteers maintains and restores all of the Clackamas country's many trails. On their website you can find directions, topographic maps and pictures of trails both known and obscure. Their hard work and dedication are much appreciated!

* **Oregon Wildflowers** (http://oregonwildflowers.org/) – Similar to Portland Hikers but with a focus on wildflowers. You can view trip reports and see some of the webmaster Greg Lief's excellent wildflower photos.

* **Northwest Waterfall Survey** (http://www.waterfallsnorthwest.com/nws/) – This website should be indispensable for those who love waterfalls. Every known waterfall in Oregon and Washington is catalogued and many are featured with full write-ups, great directions and absolutely spectacular photos.

* **Summit Post** (http://www.summitpost.org) – This is perhaps the world's greatest climbing website and is indispensable for information about mountains and the routes climbers use to summit them.

Also recommended are the following National Forest websites:
* **Siuslaw** (www.fs.usda.gov/siuslaw/) – Covers Mary's Peak (Hike 7)
* **Gifford Pinchot** (www.fs.usda.gov/giffordpinchot/) – Covers Southwest Washington (Hikes 8 – 15)
* **Mt. Hood** (www.fs.usda.gov/mthood) – Covers Mount Hood and the Clackamas (Hikes 25 – 42, 45 – 46)
* **Willamette** (www.fs.usda.gov/willamette/) – Covers the Opal Creek and Mount Jefferson areas (Hikes 43 – 50)

With all that said, let's go hiking!

Forest Park

1. Newton Road Loop
2. St. Johns Bridge Loop

1. Newton Road Loop

Distance: 4.0 mile loop
Elevation Gain: 860 feet
Season: all year
Best: all year
Pass: None
Map: Forest Park (Green Trails #426S)

Directions: Drive north from Portland on US 30, St. Helens Road to the Linnton neighborhood. Just past an intersection with NW Marina Way, 2.5 miles north of the St. Johns Bridge, look for a very small pullout on the left of the road immediately beneath some high-tension power lines. Parking may be difficult but is possible on the other side of St. Helens Road. Alternately, you may take Trimet bus #16 to a stop at the corner of NW St. Helens Road and NW Marina Way (Stop ID 10291). The trailhead is in a small roadcut beneath the power lines.

Hike: This superb hike will make you forget at times you are in Forest Park, just minutes from a busy highway inside Portland city limits. You climb through a forested jungle to the dense woods on the Wildwood Trail. You will then descend a surprisingly beautiful powerline corridor that is spangled with wildflowers in summer. There is enough to see and do on this short trek that you will likely come back again and again, all throughout the year. This is my favorite hike in the Portland area.

From a small gate next to St. Helens Road, you turn left on a rocky trail and almost immediately reach a fork. Turn left and hike on a narrow, somewhat overgrown trail that parallels St. Helens Road. While the road noise encroaches onto the trail, the forest is attractive. After a quarter mile the trail rounds a bend and enters Newton Creek's steep, jungle canyon. Look for loads of salmonberries hanging over the trail in spring. Your senses are literally overwhelmed with green (for most of the year, at least) as you parallel a trickling creek to your left. This is one of the most attractive spots in all of Forest Park and virtually nobody knows of it. Sadly, you only have this canyon to enjoy for a quarter mile, after which you cross Newton Creek and begin climbing out of the canyon on an old roadbed.

Begin climbing into more attractive forest from here as you approach the Wildwood Trail. In summer look for oceans of orange tiger lilies on the sides of the road. The trail levels out and enters deeper forest, finally meeting the Wildwood at a well-traveled intersection 1.3 miles from the trailhead. If you have ever hiked the Wildwood Trail, you will not be surprised to see that this section is much like the rest of the Wildwood – wide and gradual and continually winding in and out of side canyons through attractive forest. Stay on this popular hiking and jogging path for 1.15 miles. Watch your step as this section of the Wildwood is particularly popular with spotted leopard slugs – don't crush them!

9

When you reach a set of high tension lines, round a bend and meet the BPA Road in a section of Forest Park known as Hole-In-The-Park. Turn right on this old road and travel through a deforested power line corridor. Normally such a place would not be attractive for hiking, but in fact the deforestation has brought in other attractions – copious amounts of wild raspberries, thimbleberries and salmonberries as well as even more copious amounts of wildflowers. Depending on the season, look for pink foxglove and fireweed, purple Oregon iris and red columbine, among others. Ignore a trail junction with Firelane 12 at 0.35 mile from the Wildwood. After 0.6 mile underneath the power lines, reach a trail junction that is not obvious. To return to your car (or bus stop), turn right; to explore more of this part of Forest Park, turn left and immediately reach an unexpected picnic area complete with two tables below two sets of power lines.

While the view is obstructed you can see down to the confluence of the Columbia and Willamette Rivers at Sauvie Island and across Vancouver, Washington to Mount Saint Helens and Mount Rainier. This is a great lunch spot despite the power lines. The road to your left goes nowhere and does not reach St. Helens Road, so return to the junction and turn left on BPA Road. You will switchback steeply 0.9 mile down to a reunion with the Newton Road Trail and your trailhead. The section of road just above the trailhead is in fact *very* steep, so trekking poles are recommended. If you came by bus, turn right and walk down St. Helens road about 150 feet to the nearest bus stop.

Other hiking options:
Remember the road leaving the picnic area to your left that goes nowhere? It does in fact, go nowhere. However, if you have some extra time, it is well worth the effort to follow this road for 0.3 mile downhill into a gorgeous, lush forest that seems to hang over the path like something out of *The Hobbit*. This is a particularly attractive setting on a foggy day in winter. When you reach a junction with Firelane 13A, turn around and hike back uphill towards the picnic area. You cannot descend any further without bushwhacking as both roads dead-end in small clearings ringed by tangles of blackberry bushes.

If you have any more time, you can add an additional loop through more attractive forest by connecting the Wildwood Trail and two firelanes with an intersection at Hole-In-The-Park. To add this loop, continue straight on the Wildwood past the junction with BPA Road another 0.9 mile to a junction with Firelane 15. Turn right and descend steeply 0.4 mile to a junction with Firelane 12, and turn right again for 0.5 mile on this wide former road to climb back up to the Hole-In-The-Park junction. Then turn left on BPA Road to finish the loop. This loop adds an additional 1.8 miles and 400 feet of elevation gain to your hike.

2. St. Johns Bridge Loop

Ridge Trail Loop: 3.9 mile loop (+1.6 miles on the St. Johns bridge)
Longer loop distance: 7.2 mile loop (+1.6 miles on the St. Johns bridge)
Elevation Gain: 900 feet
Season: all year
Best: all year
Pass: None
Map: Forest Park (Green Trails #426S)

Directions: From Portland, drive north on St. Helens Road (US 30) to the St. Johns Bridge. Although the hike is in Forest Park on the west side of the Willamette River, it is easier to find parking on the east side of the river. Therefore, at signs for the St. Johns Bridge, turn left and drive up Bridge Avenue to a light. Turn right to cross the bridge and once across, duck onto neighborhood side streets to find parking. You can also take Trimet buses **4** (*Fessenden*), **16** (*Front Ave / St. Helens Rd / Sauvie Island*), **44** (*Mock's Crest*) and **75** (*Lombard*) to St. Johns. The #16 bus to Sauvie Island stops on the west side of the bridge at the intersection of Bridge Avenue and Springville Road while the other buses only stop in downtown St. Johns. The #16 bus runs far less frequently than the other three, unfortunately. If you take this bus, wait until after the bus does its loop through St. Johns to signal so that you can get off closest to the trailhead. Watch out when crossing Bridge Avenue – it is **extremely** busy at most times of the day. For more information about public transit to St. Johns, consult Trimet's website at http://www.trimet.org

Hike: Only 15 minutes from downtown Portland, this slice of wilderness in the city of Portland is ideal for hiking at any time of year. If you are not in the mood to leave the city you can still have a secluded, forested experience that is on par with many hikes in the Cascades. While you will not find total solitude, you will find the trails here less crowded than elsewhere in Forest Park. As there are over 70 miles of trails in Forest Park many loop and shuttle options are possible; here you will find a short option and a long option, both of which are exceptional hikes in any season.

Begin in St. Johns on the east side of the St. Johns Bridge. This architectural masterpiece spans high above the Willamette River, offering spectacular views of the Portland area and beyond. To the south, Mount Hood and downtown Portland shimmer in the sun; Mount Adams is visible straight through the arches of the bridge to the northeast; and to the north is Mount Saint Helens with Mount Rainier peeking over a ridge to the left. After crossing the bridge, cross Bridge Avenue and turn left on the gravel sidewalk. 100 feet down the sidewalk, you will find the Ridge Trail climbing above the highway via a set of staircases. Turn right here and begin climbing above the busy street.

The Ridge Trail is never steep but climbs almost continuously for 0.6 mile to a junction with Leif Erikson Drive. When you reach this busy biker and runner thoroughfare, turn right. Although you will see plenty of trail runners and cyclists, this part of Forest Park is generally much quieter than the crowded southern end of the Park. Walk on Leif Erikson for 0.9 mile to a wide junction with Springville Road. Turn left here.

Begin walking up Springville Road, which like Leif Erikson Drive, is closed to car traffic. One of the oldest roads in the state of Oregon, Springville Road was surveyed and built in the 1850s to help bring produce and wares from the farms of the Tualatin Valley down to the community of Springville along the Willamette River. Hike uphill about 0.4 mile to a junction with the Wildwood Trail. Continue straight on Springville, climbing another 0.3 mile to a junction with Firelane 7 near Springville Road's upper trailhead. Turn left on wide Firelane 7 and almost immediately begin descending. After less than a tenth of a mile, you reach a junction with the Hardesty Trail and are met with a whole series of choices. So far you have hiked about 2.2 miles (plus another 0.8 mile of walking from St. Johns). You could easily turn left on the Hardesty Trail and descend 0.56 mile to Leif Erikson, where you then turn right and hike another 0.56 mile to the Ridge Trail and a return to the bridge. A better option would be to continue downhill another quarter mile on Firelane 7 to a junction with the Ridge Trail. Turn left and hike downhill 1.35 mile to the St. Johns Bridge, completing a fun and easy 3.9 mile loop (with the bridge crossing, this comes out to 5.7 miles).

For a longer loop, continue past the junction with the Hardesty Trail about 300 feet to a poorly-marked junction with the Trillium Trail on your right. This steep, muddy trail drops almost 400 feet in a short quarter mile to the Wildwood Trail.

The Wildwood dips in and out of ferny glades through deep forest for the entirety of its 30 mile length and this stretch is no exception. You won't gain much elevation, so you can hike on cruise control here and instead focus your attention on the sights and sounds of Forest Park. It is particularly lovely to come here in the winter, when the foot traffic is minimal and the silence almost overwhelming. You will stay on the Wildwood for 1.9 miles until you reach a junction with Firelane 5. Here, turn left and descend a quick switchback to a junction with Leif Erikson, 4.6 miles from the beginning of your hike. Turn left on Leif Erikson and hike 2.1 miles to the Ridge Trail, which dives downhill to your right. Turn right and hike 0.6 mile back to the St. Johns Bridge. Along the way be sure to stop at a viewpoint just before you reach the St. Johns Bridge. Here, the view opens up to the full span of the bridge, backed by north Portland and Mounts Rainier, Saint Helens and Adams. This is one of the premium photography spots in the city of Portland and is always worth a stop.

Coast and Coast Range

3. Upper Salmonberry River
4. Lower Salmonberry River
5. Netarts Spit
6. Valley Of The Giants
7. Mary's Peak

3. Upper Salmonberry River

Distance: 9 miles out and back
Elevation Gain: 600 feet
Season: all year
Best: April – May, October
Pass: None
Map: None needed.

Directions: For the upper trailhead, follow US 26 west of Portland for 36.2 miles to Timber Junction. Turn left on NW Timber Road and stay on this road for 3 miles to the small town of Timber. At a junction with Cochran Road, turn right and continue first on pavement and then gravel. 1.5 miles from the junction you pass Reehers Camp. 6.5 miles from the junction in Timber, turn left at an unmarked junction on Standard Grade and immediately pull into a large parking turnaround. If you pass Cochran Pond (on your left) you've gone too far. To reach the actual trailhead, walk south on Standard Grade Road approximately 500 feet to where it crosses the railroad tracks. Turn right to begin your hike.

Hike: Hike a former rail line through tunnels and over trestles into the heart of a spectacular canyon deep in the Coast Range – how much more adventure can you find in the Coast Range? Once part of the Tillamook Railroad's coast-to-Portland rail line, massive washouts in 2006 wrought so much damage in this remote canyon that they will likely never be repaired. The way, however, is better than it ever has been for foot travel. Today, the spectacular Salmonberry River canyon now sees no trains and almost no human use save the occasional hiker. Their loss is your gain.

Begin by hiking down Standard Grade Road 500 feet to the railroad crossing. Turn right here and you will soon reach Cochran Pond. This is a tranquil spot – you may see all sorts of wildlife here, from ducks to elk to herons. Continue downhill as you begin to descend into the canyon of Pennoyer Creek, a tributary of the Salmonberry. As you hike into increasingly wild country, note how nature is retaking this canyon; while it has only been 7 years since the washouts, the sprouting of trees and brush would lead you to believe the line has been abandoned for 20 years or more.

Approximately 3 miles from the trailhead, reach the first of two tunnels. A headlamp is recommended, as the tunnel is long and curvy. When you exit the other side of the tunnel, you come almost immediately to the first of two large trestles, a high crossing of Baldwin Creek. The next mile is high adventure, as you cross Baldwin Creek and begin following the Salmonberry River. The damage begins as you cross a set of tracks above a washout below you; while the way is not dangerous, watch your step! Begin winding into the side canyon of Wolf Creek and come to the first major washout at 4 miles from the trailhead. Here the ground failed beneath the tracks, causing the unsupported ties to fall to the canyon bottom. Luckily, there is an escape path around the washout to your left.

Just after the washout, reach the second tunnel. This one is much shorter and no lamp is necessary.

Upon exiting the second tunnel, reach the second major trestle, spanning high above Wolf Creek. This makes for a great place to turn around, as the railroad begins to descend through heavy blowdown to reunite with the Salmonberry River. The going gets much tougher from here. If you keep going, you will eventually reach a huge washout on the river itself about halfway down. The lower end of the canyon is described in Hike 4.

Other Hiking Options:
If you have a lot of energy or the ability to arrange a car shuttle you can continue downstream into the canyon of the Salmonberry River. Deep in the canyon you will encounter multiple washouts on the rail line, lots of brush and absolutely gorgeous scenery that makes braving the first two worth it. Six miles from the Wolf Creek Bridge you will exit a tunnel into the hamlet of Enright, with two (sometimes inhabited) houses, a long series of empty metal boxcars and a large water tank. The rest of the route downstream is described in Hike 4.

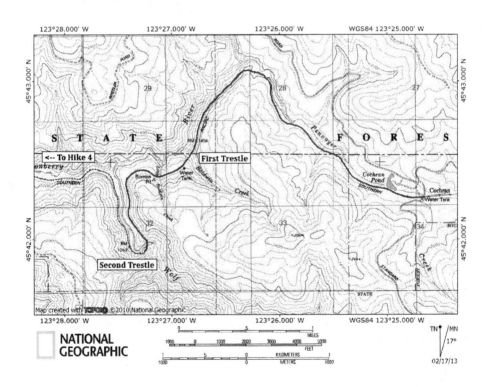

4. Lower Salmonberry River

Distance: 10.2 miles out and back
Elevation Gain: 280 feet
Season: all year
Best: April – May, October
Pass: None
Map: None needed.

Directions: Follow US 26 west of Portland for 54 miles to a junction with Lower Nehalem Road. Just a half mile from the junction, turn left at a stop sign and continue 12 miles on Lower Nehalem Road (which becomes Foss Road 2 miles before the trailhead) to a bridge over the Salmonberry River. Where the tracks cross the road, this is your trailhead. Look for a pullout on the left side of the road to park.

Hike: Much like the upper canyon of the Salmonberry River (Hike 3), here you can hike on a former rail line aside a spectacularly beautiful river. In 2006 a massive winter storm deluged the Coast Range, causing extensive flooding and washouts in its wake. The rail line along the Salmonberry River was damaged so badly that it will likely never be repaired, leaving the canyon the domain of the occasional hiker and a handful of fishermen. On this hike, you will experience the charm of the lower Salmonberry River canyon, following the river closely over trestles and past decaying railroad machinery. It's tons of fun!

Begin by hiking east from the trailhead into the canyon. This section of railway is becoming grown in (this is a continual problem on this hike) but you can usually avoid the brush by hiking alongside the railway. After just 0.6 mile, you will cross the Salmonberry on a low trestle; from this point on, you will follow the river at a very close distance. Cross cascading Buick Creek at 1.2 miles and just 0.3 mile later, cross the Salmonberry again on a historic 1923 trestle. The railway just before the bridge here has washed out but there is an escape path to the right. Be careful!

Once across the river the trail becomes particularly brushy, with one section so bad a 0.2 mile escape path has been trampled into the forest to the left of the railway. Bringing a set of hedge clippers would not be a bad idea here as the former rail line is maintained only by hikers – others will appreciate a bit of maintenance! At 3.6 miles from the trailhead, reach Belfort Rock Pit on your left. There is a decent campsite located next to an old piece of train machinery. Just 0.4 mile later, cross the Salmonberry on another historic trestle. The river here is particularly beautiful as it curves through a mossy, forested gorge.

At 4.8 miles from the trailhead, a large water tank announces your arrival at Enright, formerly a small community along the rail line. Stay on the tracks here as there are two houses that are still occupied on occasion. This area has also been logged recently and the resulting clearcut is quite the eyesore. A large series of open metal boxcars still rest along the track to your left. At the far end of Enright is your first tunnel of the day. Hike through the tunnel to a flat spot above the river; this is a fantastic spot for lunch and marks a great turnaround spot. You can, of course, continue another 10.7 miles upstream to the upper trailhead described in hike 3; unless you can arrange a time-consuming shuttle, it is best to return the way you came.

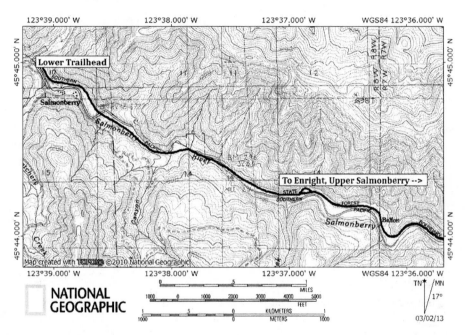

5. Netarts Spit

Distance: 10.0 miles out and back
Elevation Gain: zero
Season: All year
Best: January – March
Pass: Pay $5 to enter Cape Lookout State Park.
Map: None needed.

Directions: From Portland, drive US 26 for 20 miles to a junction with OR 6. Take the left exit here onto OR 6 and travel 51 miles to Tillamook. At a junction with US 101 in downtown Tillamook, turn left for 2 blocks to a junction with OR 131 (3rd Street / Netarts Highway). Turn right here and leave Tillamook, following signs for the Three Capes Scenic Route and Cape Lookout State Park. After 5 miles, ignore signs for Netarts and turn left on Whiskey Creek Road. Drive this road for another 5.2 miles to the south entrance of Cape Lookout State Park. Turn right into the park and find a parking spot in the lower parking lot (not the campground), which provides beach access.

Hike: There are very few secluded beaches on the northern Oregon coast; perhaps the most secluded is Netarts Spit, part of Cape Lookout State Park west of Tillamook. The hike out to the tip of the spit is excellent any time of the year but is especially recommended on a stormy day in late winter, when this lonely strip of beach can feel like the edge of the world.

Set out from the State Park and head immediately to the beach. Turn right and head north, staying just above the tide. This is your route. Keep your eyes on the tide but also on your feet as agates and sand dollars are strewn about the spit. If you're paying attention you'll probably come away with a backpack filled with rocks, shells and full sand dollars. This is among the loneliest stretches of beach on the North Coast for reasons I cannot comprehend – it's beautiful!

Heading north you'll have in full view Three Arch Rocks, three beautiful rock arches just off the shore of the beach north of the spit. Sometimes when the sun peeks out after a rain storm here a rainbow will form over the arch, framing it in a most photogenic way. Don't leave your camera at home! After approximately five miles you'll reach the end of the spit at a long, rounded beach. Look across the bay to the town of Netarts with its vacation homes. Seals often bark loudly in the bay. Sit back and enjoy the scene.

The only way back is down the beach as impassible mud flats block the bay side of the spit. You probably won't mind a bit, as the views are even nicer looking south on your return. Large and scenic trees you didn't notice the first time bend for the wind. The sand bluffs hold copious amounts of driftwood, perfect for a quick rest. The rocky coastline of Cape Lookout frames the long stretch of beach perfectly. When you reach the end of the beach at a small headland, turn left to return to your car.

Other Hiking Options:
Bluff View: If you wish to add a bit of elevation gain you can park at a pullout on a bluff 1.5 miles south of the park entrance on 3 Capes Scenic Route. An unmarked trail on the west (right) side of the road leads to an intersection with the Oregon Coast Trail. Turn right and rapidly descend a sometimes muddy trail with excellent views of Netarts Spit. After 0.75 mile the trail bottoms out in a lovely and dark forest above the beach. On your left is a view of a rugged scene: many ephemeral waterfalls (in winter and early spring) crashing down off the cliffs above directly into the ocean. It is an awesome sight to behold! From here you'll pass the rental cabins in the State Park. Please respect the privacy of the occupants and stay on the trail! Proceed from here to the beach. Before choosing to hike in this way remember that the elevation gain comes on the hike out – when you may be tired. Plan accordingly.

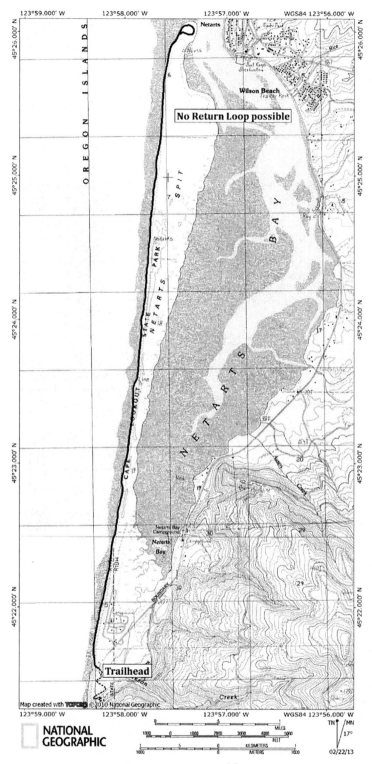

6. Valley of the Giants

Distance: 1.3 mile partial loop
Elevation Gain: 800 feet
Season: April – October
Best: April – October
Pass: None
Map: BLM Salem map

Directions: Begin your expedition by driving to the small town of Falls City. From Portland drive Interstate 5 south 47 miles to Salem. Leave the interstate at exit 260A, following signs for OR 99E. Follow this highway through Salem until you reach downtown. When you reach a junction with OR 22, turn right and cross the Willamette River. Stay on OR 22 for 10 miles to a junction with OR 223. Turn a slight left onto OR 223 towards the town of Dallas. When you arrive in Dallas, turn left to continue on OR 223, following signs for Kings Valley. Continue on OR 223 as it turns through town and drive south of Dallas 6.5 miles to a junction with Falls City Road. Turn right and follow this paved route for 4.5 miles to the bridge in Falls City. From Falls City is where it gets...interesting.

From Falls City, turn left onto Bridge Street and cross the bridge over the Luckiamute River. It is advised that you reset your trip odometer here. From here on out, these directions should work for you:

- Continue on Bridge Street, trading pavement for gravel, for approximately 15 miles through clearcut forest to the abandoned town of Valsetz.
- Reach a large "Y" intersection that may feature a company logging sign here; turn right.
- Drive for 2 miles more around the remains of Valsetz Lake to an awkward curve near the concrete remnants of a building. Bear to the left, cross a short bridge and fork to the right.
- Drive around what used to be Valsetz Lake for 1 mile to a Y junction, where you turn right. Continue around the remains of the lake for another 2.5 miles to another Y junction, where you bear right again.
- Continue another 1.6 miles to a junction at a bridge – do not cross this bridge, keeping to the left instead. The Siletz River will be on your right for the next 4 miles.
- After another 2.7 miles, you will cross a concrete bridge over a side stream. Continue another 0.5 mile to a Y junction, where you will fork to the right on the lower road.
- Just 0.1 mile later you will cross the Siletz River on a wooden trestle. The river will now be to your left. Past the bridge drive another 0.3 mile to a Y junction and fork to the right (uphill) on Road 100.
- Drive another 0.3 mile to yet another Y junction, this one with a traffic island. Fork to the left.
- Continue 1.4 miles to a metal bridge over a side creek. Continue straight, keeping the river to your left. Drive 1.7 more miles to a guardrail bridge,

where you keep straight yet again. Continue another 1.3 miles to a well-marked junction with S-Line Road, where you again keep straight. By now you should be seeing small "VOG" signs at almost every intersection. These mark your way to Valley of the Giants.

- Continue straight 0.2 mile to a concrete bridge. Cross the bridge and continue straight another 0.2 mile to another bridge, this one over the river. Cross the bridge, and from this point on the river is to your right.
- Continue straight 1.1 mile to a final Y junction, and fork to the right. You will drive 0.4 mile more to the trailhead, located on your right. You have now traveled nearly 15 miles from Valsetz and almost 30 from Falls City.

Though you are much closer to Lincoln City than you are to Falls City, do **NOT** attempt to reach the trailhead from the west – these roads are gated logging roads that do not allow public access. If you want to be as sure as can be of reaching Valley of the Giants, please contact the Salem division of the Bureau of Land Management or see my website for even more detailed directions. Getting there might seem like an ordeal but trust me, **IT IS WORTH IT**.

Hike: Provided you can get to the trailhead, Valley of the Giants is undoubtedly the best old-growth hike in Oregon's Coast Range. Words cannot describe the emotions one feels standing among such giants – this is Oregon's; answer to California's famous redwood groves. You will appreciate it all the more after driving through an ocean of clearcuts for 90 minutes on gravel roads to get there. Though the drive is circuitous and the hike less than 2 miles long, every Oregonian should make the trek to Valley of the Giants at least once. It does not just live up to the hype; it exceeds it. Please plan this trip for a weekend day to avoid the caravan of logging trucks that rumble up and down these roads on weekdays! Save this hike for a rainy Sunday in spring or fall.

From the trailhead, set off downhill through a forest of huge, moss-covered firs for half a mile to a metal bridge over the Siletz River. On your way down, look for a couple of giant Douglas firs, including one 8-foot thick behemoth that is well-loved. When you reach the river, cross the bridge and turn right on a footpath heading upstream and into tremendous, primordial forest. The path ascends through some of the most stunning old-growth you'll see anywhere in Oregon. Your eyes will be drawn to the sky by some of the giants in this grove; all in all this 51-acre preserve contains some of Oregon's largest Douglas firs. Stop to take in the trees and snap dozens of

photos. The trail slowly ascends through the grove before seemingly ending at the foot of a downed goliath; this is the legendary "Big Guy", the record Douglas fir with a circumference of 36 feet that finally fell in 1981. Rather than detouring around the tree, the slender folks in your group can follow a trail through a narrow cut in the tree to the continuation of the trail on the other side. This is a really cool stop and is highly recommended. Take your pack off first!

After you have had your fun going back and forth through the tree and after you have taken another two or three dozen photos, continue on the trail this time heading slightly downhill. This part of the path continues past more giant trees before reuniting with the trail near the bridge. At the picnic table near the bridge a path leads down to a lovely rock bench next to a particularly scenic section of the Siletz River; this is an exceptional spot to lean back and watch the river, eat and take in the sights and sounds. Return the way you came.

Other Hiking Options:
Falls City Falls: No visit to Falls City is complete without visiting its namesake falls on the Little Luckiamute River. To find Falls City Falls, you have two options. The safest route is to go back to Bridge Ave on your way out of Falls City. Just before crossing the bridge (or just after if you are headed towards Valley of the Giants), turn left onto Parry Street and drive a tenth of a mile to a small park with a view of the falls. For a better view but a rougher access, instead cross the bridge back over the river into town and turn left onto Mitchell Street. After a tenth of a mile, look for a steep dirt road angling off to the left. Park and walk down to a face-to-face view of the falls.

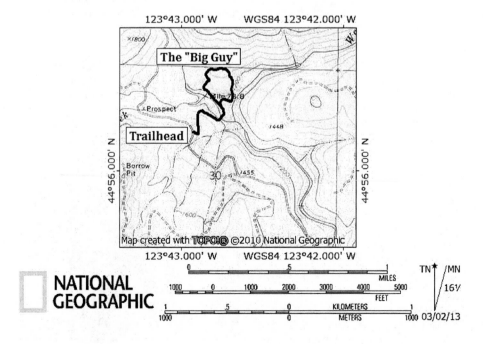

7. Mary's Peak

Distance: 9.0 miles
Elevation Gain: 2000 feet
Season: May – November
Best: May - June
Pass: None
Map: None available

Directions: From Portland, drive I-5 south 65 miles to exit 234B. Following signs for US 20 merge onto the highway and drive 12 miles to Corvallis. Turn right and stay on US 20 another 7 miles to a junction with OR 34. Keep to your right on US 20 another 1.7 miles to a junction with Woods Creek Road. Turn right and follow paved road that eventually turns to gravel. The road ends 7.5 miles from the highway at a gate and parking area. The trail is on your left.

Hike: The highest point in the Oregon Coast Range, Mary's Peak commands a view from the Pacific to the Cascades. Wildflowers grow in amazing abundance on the summit's enormous, humped meadow. Mary's Peak is a place every Oregonian should visit at least once and thanks to a paved road that leads to the summit meadows, every Oregonian *can* visit. So why include such a popular place in a book devoted to unpopular hikes? The secret, naturally, is that you can hike to the summit on a beautiful, quiet trail amidst rare coastal old-growth, and if you time your visit for a weekday or come later in the year (if you don't mind missing the flower show), you might just have the summit to yourself too.

Begin at a gate and almost immediately fork to the right on the well-marked trail. Hike through a lovely Douglas fir forest with a verdant carpet of moss. In May and June the Oregon iris grows profusely here, rewarding hikers of this lower trail. Keep a look out for other flowers as well, including yellow monkeyflower and red columbine, both of which are almost as abundant here as the iris. After 0.5 mile, reach a junction and turn right. Almost immediately begin climbing via a series of switchbacks. While never steep, the climbing is constant for the next 3 miles as you work up the forested north ridge of Mary's Peak. Here you will find some of the larger trees left in this part of the Coast Range – while not in national forest, they are instead protected because they are in Corvallis' municipal watershed. Consider this while you hike.

At 3.5 miles from the trailhead meet a junction with the Tie Trail at a bench. Turn right here and soon level out in a lovely noble fir forest that slowly opens up to offer vistas of the vast summit meadows of Mary's Peak. Just 0.5 mile later reach the large parking lot at the upper end of the North Ridge Trail. On summer weekends this is a busy place. Spot the road heading up the vast green meadow before you and follow it as it curls around to the weather station at the summit, some 4,097 feet above sea level. The view is breathtaking – on a clear day you can see from Mount Adams in Washington to Diamond Peak, south of the Three Sisters, and from a thin sliver of the Pacific Ocean to the Cascades and over the entirety of the Willamette Valley. At your feet is a carpet of larkspur, paintbrush, lupine and dozens of other wildflowers. Despite the summit's weather station equipment this is one of the most inspiring places in the state of Oregon. If the weather is threatening, this is one of Oregon's windiest, most inhospitable places. Plan your hike for a sunny day and bring a picnic! Return the way you came.

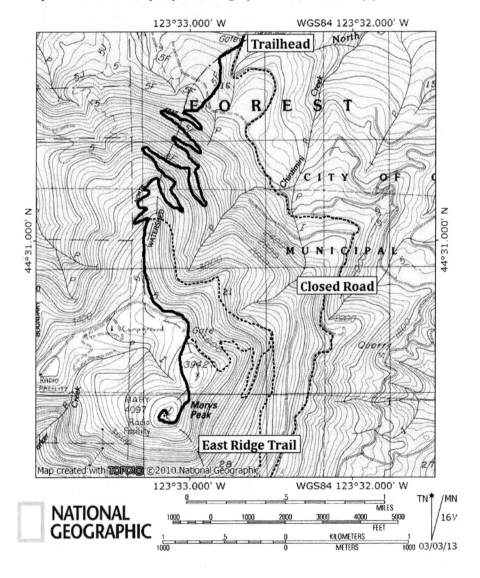

Southwest Washington

8. **Silver Star Mountain via Starway**
9. **Black Hole Falls**
10. **Goat Marsh Lake**
11. **Butte Camp Trail**
12. **Cave Falls / Curly Creek Falls**
13. **Quartz Creek**
14. **Indian Racetrack / Red Mountain**
15. **Lookingglass Lake**

8. Silver Star Mountain via Starway

Distance: 12 miles out and back
Elevation Gain: 3,500 feet
Season: June – October
Best: late June – early August
Pass: None
Map: Washington DNR Map

Directions: From Portland, drive north on Interstate 5 past Vancouver. At exit 9, leave the freeway on WA 502 and drive 7.7 miles to Battle Ground. From the junction of WA 502 and WA 503 in Battle Ground, turn left and drive 5.6 miles on WA 503 to a junction with Rock Creek Road, signed for Lucia and Moulton Falls. Turn right and drive 8.5 miles to a road signed for Sunset Campground. Turn right here and drive another 7.5 paved miles to Sunset Campground. Turn right at the campground on FR 41 and cross a bridge. Turn left on the other side and drive 4 gravel miles to the unmarked trailhead on your right at a junction with often-gated FR 4107. The last two miles are potholed and rocky but manageable for low-clearance vehicles if you drive slowly.

Hike: To reach the flower gardens and expansive views on the summit of Silver Star Mountain, you can go the easy way or you can go the Starway. Bad jokes aside, there are five routes to the summit and the Starway Trail is by far the most difficult of the five. This primitive mining trail compensates for its difficulty by offering the easiest road access of the five and spectacular views of the rugged north face of Silver Star and elusive Star Falls. Even better, you are likely to be alone for much of this hike despite being less than 30 miles from downtown Portland.

Begin by walking down FR 4107 0.5 mile to a metal hiker bridge over Copper Creek. If the gate is open you can also drive down here as the road is not much worse than the one you drove in on but remember – should the gate close while you are hiking, you are stuck. Cross the bridge and turn left on a rougher continuation of the road for 0.3 mile to a junction sometimes marked by a cairn. Turn right and begin hiking up the Starway. The trail climbs gradually at first as it leaves the canyon of Copper Creek. After you traverse a rockslide, the trail launches uphill and begins climbing a brutally steep clip. At first you have the benefit of a few switchbacks but soon you will find yourself hiking uphill on a trail with a 40 – 45 percent grade. Thankfully, this stretch of trail is well-maintained and forested, providing the weary hiker with cool shade even on very hot days. Approximately 2 miles from the bridge, the trail suddenly tops out almost 2,000 feet higher at a rudimentary shelter on your right. Follow flagging through the forest as you begin to climb again. Soon after, you will exit the forest for the first of many big views of the huge massif that is the north side of Silver Star.

From here you will trade forest for meadows as the rough trail lurches up steeply,

levels out and then climbs steeply to a knoll at 3.2 miles from the trailhead. For a less difficult hike, you can scramble up to the summit of the 3,977' knoll for a view almost as good as that at the summit. The flower show here is spectacular, and earlier in the summer you will be treated to a rare view of Star Falls, a pair of plunges in the canyon below. Mount Hood rises above and beside Little Baldy to your left (southeast). This is a spot worthy of a lengthy break, if not lunch.

If you are continuing, you will descend steeply through open forest and meadows until you reach a rocky viewpoint closer to Star Falls. This descent is brutal on the return trip, so avoid this hike on very hot days. From here the brushy and rough trail begins to climb steeply again, reaching a junction with the Bluff Mountain Trail almost 5 miles from the trailhead. While there are great views on the side of Little Baldy to your left, turn right for the real prize – the summit of Silver Star Mountain. The way traverses hanging meadows with tremendous wildflower displays that last from late-June into August. After 0.8 mile of spectacular meadows, reach a strange 4-way junction with the Silver Star Mountain trail and Ed's Trail. Turn left and hike this old road 0.4 mile to the open summit, where views stretch from Mount Rainier to Mount Jefferson. Portland and Vancouver are visible below you. The view is truly stunning and fully panoramic – and you will likely have to share it with many admirers, as four other trails reach this lofty perch.

When you can bear to return, remember to turn right on the Bluff Mountain Trail 0.4 mile below the summit, and then left on the signed Starway Trail 1.2 miles from the summit. Otherwise, you can arrange a car shuttle to return via another of Silver Star's trails. Road access and trail difficulty vary greatly, so do some research beforehand if this is your plan.

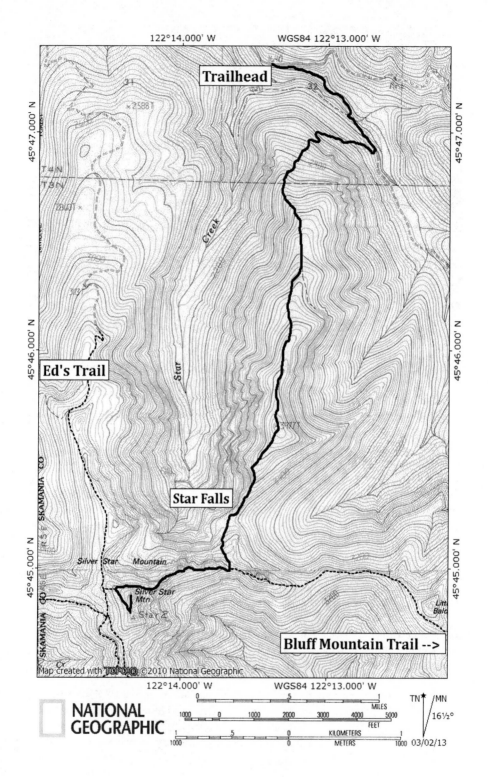

Trailhead

Ed's Trail

Star Falls

Bluff Mountain Trail -->

122°14.000' W   WGS84 122°13.000' W

45°47.000' N

45°46.000' N

45°45.000' N

NATIONAL GEOGRAPHIC

Map created with TOPO!® ©2010 National Geographic

TN / MN
16½°
03/02/13

9. Black Hole Falls

Distance: 9.4 miles out and back
Elevation Gain: 1,200 feet
Season: April – November
Best: May – June
Pass: None
Map: None available.

Directions: From Portland, drive Interstate 205 north to exit 30, just past Vancouver. Follow signs for WA 503 and Battle Ground. Keep on this paved highway through Battle Ground until you reach the small town of Amboy. Here turn right at the continuation of WA 503 and continue another 4 miles to the small community of Chelatchie. Turn right before the general store onto Healy Road.

From here drive 5.2 miles to a junction with road S 1000 on your left. Turn left here and drive 0.4 mile to another fork. Turn right here on S 1000 and drive 4.7 miles downhill, crossing the wide main fork of Siouxon Creek in the process, to another road junction. Fork to the left here (downhill), cross North Siouxon Creek and drive 1.4 miles to the trailhead at a wide parking area on your right, which is occasionally marked with a signboard.

Road S 1000 has washed out several times in the past. If you arrive at the junction with Healy Road and find S 1000 closed, continue down on Healy Road from the junction described above another 1.2 miles to a fork in the road on your left. Here a rocky gravel road climbs steeply away from Healy Road. Turn left and climb steeply on this road over a ridge and down to a wide junction with S 1000 after just 1.8 miles. From here, fork to the right on S 1000 and follow the directions above. The trailhead for North Siouxon Creek is 4.1 miles from the where this detour road joins road S 1000.

For a more detailed map of the area with all major trails and roads, consult the maps offered by the Washington State Department of Natural Resources: http://1.usa.gov/XeRW9t

Hike: An oasis in a desert of clearcuts and rough roads, Black Hole Falls is one of the most special places in the rugged canyonlands south of Mount Saint Helens. Getting there is an endeavor, but recent trailwork has made this trek much easier.

Depart from the trailhead and immediately head downhill steeply to the bottom of the canyon. From here the trail settles into a pattern of minor ups and downs. The scenery here is lovely, a classic Pacific Northwest forest of firs carpeted with ferns, oxalis and Oregon grape. While you will pass a recovering clearcut and the presence of logging is never that far removed from the trail, it does not at any point detract from this beautiful environment.
At about 1.5 miles from the trailhead reach a crossing of a side creek. The trail

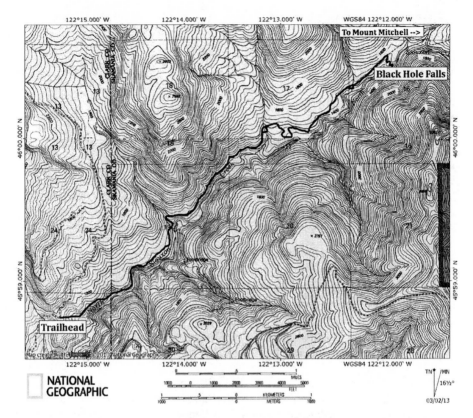

NATIONAL
GEOGRAPHIC

has been routed over a log that creates smooth passage even in high water. From here climb swiftly above this side creek and stay above North Siouxon Creek as well for a while before returning to your ups and downs about 100 vertical feet above the creek bottom. After another 1.5 miles reach a second creek crossing, this one trickier than the first. Here the trail tries to cross an unnamed side creek between tiers of a steep, sliding cascade. To make matters worse, the bank has washed out, creating a hazardous crossing. Lucky for you, recent trail work has established an escape route. After you have investigated the cascade, retrace your steps about 200 feet to a rough trail that dives down the bank. Look for a large tree with nails in it and cross the side creek here before working your way back up to the original tread. Keep this side trail in mind for the return.

Hike another 1.5 miles through more lovely forest. At the top of a small knoll reach a sign reading "Black Hole". Turn right and wind down through forest 0.2 mile to the falls. Here North Siouxon Creek explodes through a narrow crevice, fanning down 55 feet into a deep green pool ideal for swimming (but keep in mind – the water is **COLD**). This is one of the most scenic spots in this part of the Gifford Pinchot and you will likely have it all to yourself. Stay as long as you wish – you will not want to leave. When you have had your fill, return the way you came.

10. Goat Marsh Lake

Distance: 9.8 miles partial loop
Elevation Gain: 1,600 feet
Season: May – October
Best: July – August
Pass: NW Forest Pass
Map: Mount Saint Helens (Green Trails #364)

Directions: From Portland drive north on I-5 for 28 miles. Following signs for WA 503 and Cougar, leave the interstate at exit 21 and turn right at the stop light. Follow WA 503 for 28 more windy miles to Cougar. Just before reaching Cougar, curve to the left on FR 8100. Drive this paved road for 8 miles, passing Lake Merrill along the way, to a junction. Turn right on FR 8100 for just 0.2 mile to Kalama Horse Camp. Turn right and drive into the camp. Curve to the left in the camp into the day use area, and park in the lot beside the trailhead.

Hike: It is baffling why Goat Marsh Lake is overlooked. Set in ancient forest in the shadow of bulky Goat Mountain, it may be the only lake near Mount Saint Helens with a reflection of the volcano – and it happens to be less than a mile on a well-maintained trail from a gravel road. Despite all it has to offer, Goat Marsh Lake remains an obscure destination. On this longer hike from Kalama Horse Camp, you can discover what others are missing. Furthermore, this is an excellent destination on a rainy day; although you cannot see Mount Saint Helens, the lake takes on a primeval feeling reminiscent of the North Cascades.

Begin at the Kalama Horse Camp. The trail departs south from the Horse Camp and immediately reaches a confusing junction. Left is the most direct route here (see the return trip) but for a more scenic loop with a bit more elevation gain, continue straight on what is now the Cinnamon Trail (238A). You will quickly reach a bridge over the beautiful Kalama River. Continue straight past a junction with an informal trail headed right to Kalama Falls (almost 4 miles downriver – don't bother) and begin bending left into ancient forest above the Kalama River. Follow the river at a distance for approximately 1 mile until you switchback to your right out of the canyon. Though never steep, you will gain 800 feet in relatively short order. At the last switchback you will notice you are actually on an old road. When you reach a very obvious roadcut through a rockslide, turn around for a noble view of Mount Saint Helens. Continue on this old road until you meet a real road. While the Cinnamon Trail continues straight up the slope, turn left. Hike down this seldom-used road (FR 8122) for 1 mile back down to the canyon bottom. Cross the Kalama River again, pass a junction with the Toutle Trail (238) to continue to a junction with the Kalama Ski Trail (231) on your right. Turn right and hike 100 yards to a crossing of FR 8100.

Once across the road, look for the continuation of the Kalama Ski Trail at the far right end of a gravel turnaround. The trail cuts into the forest and climbs gradually for 1.5 miles (follow the blue diamonds on the trees!) to a junction with

the Goat Marsh Lake trail. Turn left and hike 0.5 mile through ancient forest to the lake. Despite the low elevation (3,000 feet), snow lingers here well into June. When you reach the lake, views emerge of Butte Camp Dome (Hike 11) and then Mount Saint Helens. At first the volcano is hidden from sight but as you hike around the lake, the mountain is revealed – and the view is stunning. Be sure to hike past the end of the lake for a view of the vast marsh that is the source of the lake's name. Elk are a common sight here in the evening. Goat Mountain looms huge over long, exceedingly green wetlands – this place has a mystical feeling!

When you are finished with the lake, return the way you came (back on the Goat Marsh Trail, right on the Kalama Ski Trail to FR 8100 and across to the side road you hiked on) back to the second crossing of the Kalama River on FR 8122. You could hike back the exact way you came, but there is a shorter, easier alternative. Just before the road crosses the river, turn right on the Toutle Trail (238). Follow the river from above as you skirt the edge of an ashy, rocky bluff. The Toutle Trail has repeatedly washed out over the years, forcing a re-route of the trail onto the Kalama Ski Trail well above the riverbank for most of this stretch. If you look down from the ashy bluffs above the river, you can see why maintaining a riverside trail eventually proved to be impossible here. After 1 mile, reach a junction with the Toutle Trail. Turn left here and switchback down to the river. At long last, you are free to follow the riverbank! Hike downstream another mile to a reunion with the Ski Trail – turn left here and hike a couple hundred yards to the Cinnamon Trail junction. Turn right here to hike back to your car.

Other hiking options:
Goat Marsh Lake via FR 8123: You can also hike to Goat Marsh Lake from a trailhead near Blue Lake. To find this trailhead, continue on FR 81another 3 miles from Kalama Horse Camp to where the pavement ends. Continue 0.6 mile of gravel to a junction. Turn left on FR 8123 following signs for Blue Lake and drive 0.6 mile to the poorly-marked trailhead on your left. There is room to park 1 – 2 cars on the left shoulder of the road. The Kalama Ski Trail departs here and descends 0.2 mile to a signed junction with the Goat Marsh Lake Trail. Turn right and hike 0.8 mile to the lake.

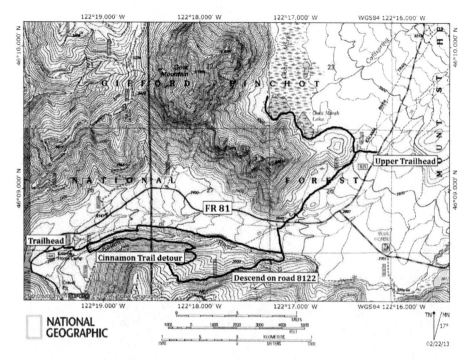

11. Butte Camp

Distance: 7.4 miles out and back
Elevation Gain: 1,600 feet
Season: July – October
Best: July – August
Pass: NW Forest Pass
Map: Mount Saint Helens (Green Trails #364)

Directions: From Portland drive north on I-5 for 28 miles. Following signs for WA 503 and Cougar, leave the interstate at exit 21 and turn right at the stop light. Follow WA 503 for 28 more winding miles to Cougar. 3 miles later WA 503 becomes FR 90. Follow this forest highway another 3.2 miles to a junction with FR 83 and signs for Mount Saint Helens. Turn left and drive 3 miles north towards the volcano to a junction with FR 81. Turn left again and drive 3 gravel miles to a small parking area at Redrock Pass.

Hike: The 1980 eruption of Mount Saint Helens obliterated the north side of the mountain and everything around it. The south side of the mountain saw less, though still significant damage. Many areas were spared entirely while canyons experienced significant *lahars*, or volcanic mudflows. On this spectacular, little-known hike up the south flank of the volcano you can sample the best of both worlds as you trade old-growth forest for volcanism and back again.

Begin at Red Rock Pass on the Toutle Trail and immediately ascend a rise to a

vast lava field with a face-to-face view of Mount Saint Helens. In some years beargrass blankets the lava field with its fragrant white blooms. Photographers may have trouble escaping this spot. If you can, continue on the trail as it enters meadows; look for lupine, penstemon and ludicrous amounts of wild strawberry blooms in July. Enter a mossy, verdant forest and hike half a mile to a junction with the Butte Camp Trail 1.2 miles from your car. Turn right here and begin climbing steadily (though never steeply; the trail is very well-graded) through a forest of pine and mountain hemlock. Listen for woodpeckers, as they love the low pines that dominate this forest. Also note the lava bombs the mountain has deposited here over the years, lest you forget you are on an active volcano!

At 2.5 miles, reach Butte Camp, a long meadow under rocky Butte Camp Dome. Early in the season the stream running through the meadow also runs along the trail, so you might need to watch your feet. Good campsites are abundant here though you may need to wait out the mosquitoes, who love this marshy environment. You won't see the volcano, however, as it is blocked by the ridge above you. If you've come for the views, keep on the trail as it switchbacks up the slope through a dark old-growth hemlock grove draped by yellow lichen. Note the height of the lichen off the trees; this is the height of the winter snow depth. Impressive! Top out and round the bend to your left to see the mountain in front of you and a steep dropoff to your right. Watch your footing on the rocky, dusty trail. Purple phlox and yellow wallflowers cling to the hillside in dramatic fashion. After this traverse, the trail reaches an ashy plain with the volcano directly in front of you. Follow the trail 0.3 mile to a junction with the round-the-mountain Loowit Trail. This is your destination. Keep an eye out for a colony of marmots that live in the area. Mount Saint Helens looms immense above you. Return the way you came or turn left on the Loowit for a longer, optional loop (see below).

Other Hiking Options:

Sheep Canyon Loop: You can make a loop by turning left at the Loowit Trail. Turn left on the Loowit Trail for 2.3 miles to the Sheep Canyon Trail. Turn left again and descend on the rim of the canyon for 1.6 miles to a junction with the continuation of the Sheep Canyon Trail. Turn left a third time and follow the trail for 2.4 miles to Blue Lake and keep straight on the Toutle Trail for 2 miles to its junction with the Butte Camp Trail. Keep straight for another 1.3 miles to reach your car. Total hike distance: 13.3 miles with 1,700 feet elevation gain.

Note: The map below was created with software that does not show all of the trails around Mount Saint Helens. There are many trails in the area not shown here. If you wish to deviate from the itinerary above I recommend purchasing a detailed map with all current trails.

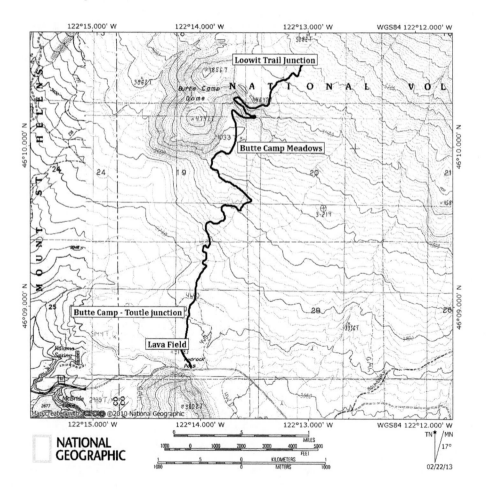

12. Cave and Curly Falls

Cave Falls distance: 2 miles out and back
Curly Falls distance: 0.5 mile out and back
Elevation Gain: 200 feet
Season: April – November
Best: April – May, October
Pass: NW Forest Pass
Map: Lone Butte (Green Trails #365)

Directions: Drive north from Portland on Interstate 5 to Woodland, WA. Take Exit 21 and turn right on WA 503. Drive east on WA 503 for 31.6 miles to the town of Cougar. Keep straight, now traveling on FR 90, for another 15 miles to a junction with FR 25. Turn right, staying on FR 90, and parallel the Lewis River for 9 more miles to the trailhead, which is signed and located on the left side of the road.

Hike: The first falls is tall and proud but the second will take your breath away, even if you can't see much of it. But there's more: giant old-growth, a wild trail descending towards a brawling, burly river and more intrigue than you'd expect to find for such an easy hike. On your way back, a second pair of waterfalls along the Lewis River beckon to be seen and heard. Sound like fun? There's enough in this area to fill days, and this is just a sample.

The trail begins in a wide pullout on the left side of the Lewis River Road. The trail descends through magnificent old-growth forest (including one giant Douglas fir over 9 feet in diameter) a quarter mile to an observation deck that looks out on 100-foot Big Creek Falls. While the trail is wide and easy to follow, don't stray too close to the canyon wall here or anywhere else on this hike – a fall would likely be fatal and it is virtually impossible to get to the canyon floor. Use caution!

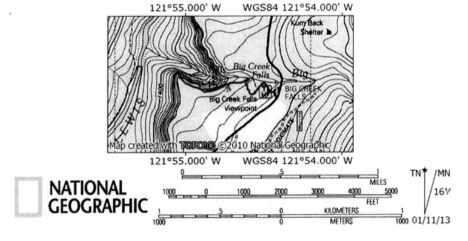

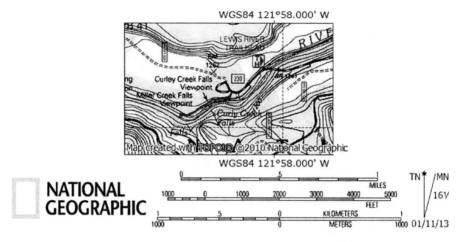

Below Big Creek Falls the tread becomes more primitive as it descends mildly. Listen for the roar of elusive Cave Falls below you on the creek; you will hear more of the falls than you can see. Look for glimpses of the falls through the trees but avoid the canyon wall. There is no safe way to get down. Follow the sound of this giant downhill 0.5 mile through a forest of hemlock and cedar to another, more rustic overlook, this time of Cave Falls. Look down over a cliff edge at parts of the falls: a punchbowl falls plunging out of a narrow slot canyon; another spigot shoots out of what seems to be a cave in the canyon wall (actually a colossal boulder), giving the waterfall its name. It is frustrating that more of Cave Falls is not visible but I'm not sure it would be possible to see more without rappelling into the canyon or sprouting wings. Exercise extreme caution near the canyon walls when attempting to get a better view of the falls.

The trail continues 0.2 mile beyond the Cave Falls viewpoint at an overlook of the Lewis River Canyon. During the rainy season look across the canyon to Hemlock Creek Falls, a slender 250-foot plunge. Alas, you cannot descend any further; instead, return the way you came.

On your way out of the canyon it is highly recommended you stop at a second pair of waterfalls along the Lewis River. Drive back FR 90 for 5 miles to a junction with FR 9039. Veer to the right (this is a sharp angle if coming from the west) for a mile, crossing the Lewis River in the process. Park in a well-signed lot to your left. A Forest Pass is required here. The trail departs from the lot and heads downhill slightly. Reach a junction after only 100 yards; follow the sound of falling water to your right, coming to lovely Curly Creek Falls in just 50 yards. The falls is a natural wonder: a 75-foot plunge into the Lewis River through a natural arch. It must be seen to be believed. Continue downstream another 100 yards to Miller Creek Falls, also on a stream emptying into the river; note how the creek divides in two just after the plunge pool. In summer the creek runs very low (as does Curly Creek) so it is recommended you visit this area in winter or spring. Return the way you came.

Other hiking options:
Lewis River Trail: 2.5 miles of hiking is not enough for many hikers. If you wish to hike more, consider hiking the Lewis River Trail. The lower section of trail departs from the bridge over FR9039 just before the Curly Creek trailhead (a section also links the Curly Creek Falls trail to the Lewis River trail – just turn left at the junction near the falls instead of right). The Lewis River Trail follows the river for 14 miles through ancient forest. This trail is popular with mountain bikers and the upper section, which passes three roaring waterfalls on the Lewis River, is very popular with hikers as well. The lower section is much quieter and features some exemplary old-growth forest. Either way, if you are looking for more ancient forest and gorgeous waterfalls, this is the place.

13. Quartz Creek

Distance: 8 miles out and back
Elevation Gain: 1,200 feet
Season: June – November
Best: July – October
Pass: NW Forest Pass
Map: Lone Butte, WA #365 (Green Trails)

Directions: Drive north from Portland on Interstate 5 to Woodland, WA. Take Exit 21 and turn right on WA 503. Drive east on WA 503 for 31.6 miles to the town of Cougar. Keep straight, now traveling on FR 90, for another 15 miles to a junction with FR 25. Turn right, staying on FR 90, and parallel the Lewis River for 17 more miles to a pullout on the right just before the road crosses Quartz Creek. The trail departs from a signboard across the road (on the left side). The trail on the right heads down to Upper Lewis River Falls.

Hike: Situated between Mount Saint Helens and Mount Adams, the Dark Divide area of the Gifford Pinchot is a secret to most Portlanders. Part of this is due to its distance from Portland but part of this obscurity is due to the Dark Divide being overshadowed by its glaciated neighbors. Nevertheless, there are many beautiful, obscure destinations in this rugged area that deserve far more attention, and Quartz Creek is among them. With giant old-growth trees, hidden waterfalls and misty forests, you won't want to miss this hike.

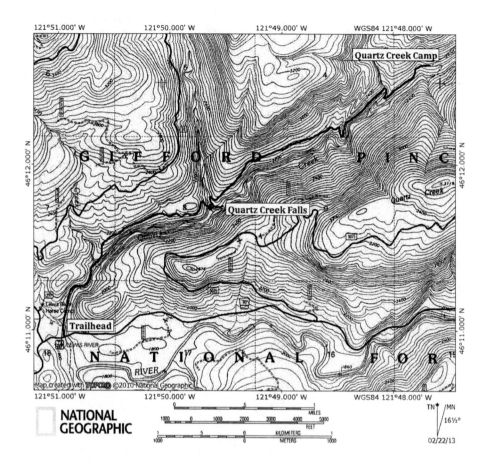

Begin at the Upper Lewis River Trailhead, where FR 90 crosses Quartz Creek. Cross the road and locate the signed trailhead on the left side of the road. You will parallel wide Quartz Creek at a close distance for the first part of the hike. After 0.7 mile you will cross Platinum Creek on a dilapidated bridge and soon begin a moderate climb up to bluffs above the creek. The trail levels out some 200 feet above Quartz Creek in verdant second-growth forest before dropping steeply to an unbridged crossing of wide, fast Straight Creek at 2 miles from the trailhead. In the summer, this is a fairly easy crossing to manage with dry feet but in the winter months is a dangerous crossing that should not be attempted.

Once you pass the crossing, take a moment to check out a fantastic and large campsite at the confluence of Straight Creek and Quartz Creek. Here's a secret: if you follow faint user paths from the campsite towards Quartz Creek for approximately 100 yards, you will arrive at a wide beach on the creek. Follow the creek another 20 yards to Quartz Creek Falls, a wide 26-foot slide with a huge splash pool. When you return to the Quartz Creek Trail, another faint trail follows Straight Creek a short ways to Straight Creek's impressive slide falls. Then return to the Quartz Creek Trail and begin climbing again, following the remains of an old mining road. After about a mile, you will top out and then begin losing elevation. The last mile of the hike is perhaps the prettiest, as the trail descends through a forest of massive old-growth Douglas firs and mountain hemlock. You may notice here how the trail weaves in and out of huge fallen trees; until very recently the trail was neglected and plagued with blowdown, but the Washington Trail Association has been faithfully restoring the trail to its past glory. Huge thanks are in order!

At 4 miles from the trailhead, reach a crossing of Snagtooth Creek. Just as with Straight Creek, this crossing is easy in the summer but in winter months is very difficult. This also makes for a convenient turnaround spot. If you feel like continuing, there is a great campsite at Quartz Creek Camp another 0.5 mile down the trail.

Return the way you came.

14. Indian Racetrack / Red Mountain

Distance: 6 miles out and back
Elevation Gain: 1,300 feet
Season: July – October
Best: September – October
Pass: NW Forest Pass
Map: Mount Adams Wilderness (USFS)

Directions: From Portland, drive east 44 miles on Interstate 84 to Cascade Locks. Leave the freeway at exit 44 and follow signs for the Bridge of the Gods. Pay $1 to cross the Columbia River and on the far side of the bridge, turn right on WA 14. Drive this highway through Stevenson and arrive at a junction with the Wind River Road 5.9 miles later. Turn left, following signs for Carson and continue on the Wind River Road 5.8 miles to the second junction with Old State Road on your right. Turn right here, and only 0.1 mile later, turn left on Panther Creek Road (FR 65). Stay on FR 65 and ignore all less major roads for 16 miles to the Falls Creek Horse Camp. You can park here or at the trailhead on the side of the road a couple hundred yards up FR 65. The trail departs to your right.

Hike: Though situated between Mount Saint Helens and Mount Adams, the Indian Heaven Wilderness does not charm and amaze with glaciated peaks and volcanic destruction but rather with tranquil ponds, vast meadows, scenic lakes and views out to its glaciated neighbors. With this hike up to the famed Indian Racetrack and then the summit of Red Mountain, you can experience the best Indian Heaven has to offer and still have time for a visit to the area's most beautiful waterfall, Panther Creek Falls. Adventurers can also hike an abandoned trail to the Basin Lakes, perhaps the most scenic place in this part of the Cascades that nobody ever visits. Avoid this area in July when the Indian Heaven Wilderness is also frequently known as the "Mosquito Heaven Wilderness".

Begin by hiking on the mostly level Indian Racetrack trail. Reach a signboard after 0.1 mile and fill out your permit. Notice the unmarked trail that departs to the left – this is the abandoned Basin Lakes Trail (see **Other Hiking Options**). Continue straight towards Indian Racetrack. Cross Falls Creek on a bridge and begin climbing through a forest covered in huckleberry. Come here in September and you might not even make it to the racetrack – these wild blueberries are prolific all throughout the Indian Heaven Wilderness. Level off and reach a scenic pond at the edge of the racetrack's meadow at 2 miles from the trailhead. Continue following the trail through the vast meadow to a junction with the Racetrack spur trail at 2.3 miles. You are now at the Indian Racetrack; here Indians raced horses for generations across this vast, rectangular meadow. A pause for reflection is highly recommended.

To continue on to the summit of Red Mountain, turn right at the junction and walk 100 feet. Look to your left for a trail with a signpost headed off into the forest to your left. When you find the trail, follow it uphill 0.8 miles to its end on rough gravel road 6048 just below the summit lookout. Follow the road past a wooden garage to its end at the lookout atop the 4,977 foot summit. Stretching out below you is the entirety of the Indian Heaven Wilderness, with the racetrack at your feet. To your left is the broken-bottle top of Mount Saint Helens. To your right is Mount Adams, looming huge above its surroundings. Behind you, to the south, is Mount Hood. The summit lookout is manned for most of the summer, but provided you came here after the mosquitoes departed, it will probably be boarded up. If you are tired, this makes for a good day hike of about 6 miles round trip. Return the way you came or add on a side trip to Basin Lakes.

Other Hiking Options:
Basin Lakes: This beautiful series of lakes nestled under Berry Mountain makes for an excellent side trip after Indian Mountain. With some patience and serious route-finding skills, you can even make a loop using the Pacific Crest Trail to connect with Indian Racetrack and Red Mountain.

To find the trail to Basin Lakes, return to the signboard just 0.1 mile from the trailhead. Here you will see a trail forking off to your left. This is the abandoned trail to Basin Lakes. Though no longer an official trail, the trail is easy to follow and is frequently flagged, which helps greatly through some of the sections of blowdown that plague the trail. What's more, the trail is for the most part straight as an arrow – if you happen to lose the trail, just plow straight through the forest and you should quickly relocate it. After approximately 2 miles you will arrive at the southern edge of Janet Lake. Backed by large trees, this beautiful pool is a great place to spend an hour or a night. The other Basin lakes are all off-trail but close at hand.

Finding the route from Basin Lakes up to the Pacific Crest Trail on the ridge above can be a real challenge. Follow the trail straight past Janet Lake over blowdown until the trail starts climbing. Sections of the climb up to the ridge are overgrown and it is very easy to lose the trail. Thankfully, this section is less than a half mile long, and should you lose the trail, you can bushwhack up this steep slope to the PCT at the ridge crest. Once you reach the PCT, turn right and hike 3.5 miles south over Berry Mountain to a junction with the Racetrack Connector Trail (171A). Turn right here and hike 0.5 mile to Indian Racetrack, where you will find the Racetrack trail. Turn right and hike back 2.3 miles to your car. The full loop is approximately 12 miles with approximately 1,800 feet of elevation gain.

If you plan on hiking the full loop, I recommend starting with the hike to Basin Lakes first. This way you can turn around and hike to the Racetrack and Red Mountain if you lose the trail to Basin Lakes. Additionally, should you lose the trail up to the PCT it is much easier to bushwhack up to the PCT than it is to bushwhack down the steep slopes from the PCT. Should you begin your loop from the Racetrack and hike up Berry Mountain to the connector trail, remember that the trail takes off from the saddle between Berry and Gifford Mountains. If you begin traversing to the right towards Gifford Mountain, you've gone too far.

Panther Creek Falls: The hike to Panther Creek Falls is not a hike; in fact, the distance from the trailhead to the waterfall viewpoint (500 feet) will take you about as much time as it will take you to read this paragraph. The falls, however, are spectacular and entirely unique. Panther Creek drops over a ledge at full strength while a spring veils down the slope adjacent to the falls. It's difficult to imagine it without seeing it for yourself. This is one of the most beautiful and peaceful places in all of southwest Washington. You can visit the falls before or after your visit to Indian Heaven; to find the falls, drive northeast on FR 65 a total of 7.4 miles from the Old State Road junction to a pullout on your right, next to a rockslide. The unmarked trail dives down the slope to your left.

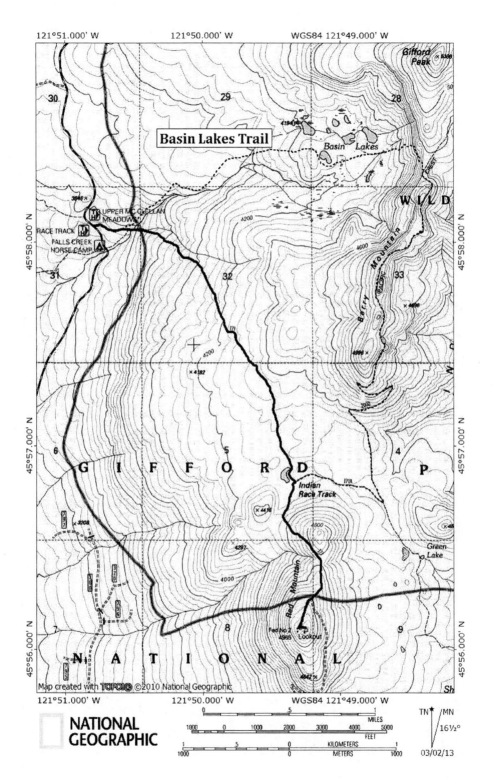

Basin Lakes Trail

15. Lookingglass Lake

Distance: 12.8 miles out and back
Elevation Gain: 1,800 feet
Season: July – October
Best: August and September
Pass: NW Forest Pass
Map: Mount Adams Wilderness (USFS)

Directions: From Portland, drive Interstate 84 to Hood River. Leave the freeway at Exit 64, marked for Mount Hood. At an interchange under the interstate, turn left, following signs for White Salmon. Cross the Columbia River on a long metal bridge with a $1 toll and at the end of the bridge, turn left at a junction with WA 14. Drive 1.5 miles to a junction with WA 141 ALT and drive this paved highway 2.2 miles to a junction with WA 141. Turn left here and drive this two-lane paved highway 19 miles to Trout Lake. At a forked junction just before downtown Trout Lake, turn right on the Mount Adams highway, FR 23. Just 1.3 miles later, turn right, following signs for the South Climb Trailhead and Bird Creek Meadows. After 0.6 mile, fork abruptly to the left onto FR 80 and follow this one-lane paved road for 3.7 miles to yet another fork. Keep right and drive on FR 8040 for 5.4 miles of washboarded gravel to Morrison Creek Forest Camp and the Shorthorn Trailhead. The dirt road inside the campground is very rough, with large buried rocks and deep ruts. Passenger car drivers are advised to park near the campground entrance wherever possible. The trailhead is at the end of the campground, where there is a small parking lot and privy.

Hike: When it comes to Mount Adams, the South Climb, Bird Creek Meadows and Killen Creek Trails get all the attention. While all three are spectacular and well worth making every effort to hike, they also require long drives on rough roads and still manage to be very, very crowded. Avoid all of this by hiking to breathtaking Lookingglass Lake on the southwest side of the volcano via the little-known Shorthorn Trail. Not only is the drive shorter and less onerous, you will also be rewarded with fantastic views of Mount Adams for much of your hike, superb wildflower displays and no crowds to speak of, anywhere on your hike. What could be better?

Before we begin, please note that this hike crosses through terrain burned in the Cascade Creek Fire in Fall 2012, just before this book went to press. I was unable to survey the damage to this hike. Before you hike to Lookingglass Lake, please call the Mount Adams Ranger Station for current trail conditions.

Begin by hiking the Shorthorn Trail. Originally constructed as a way trail for sheepherders in the late 19th Century, the grade of this trail alternates between almost-level and steep. Start out with a nearly-level section, climbing gradually amidst beargrass in a forest of lodgepole pine. Abundant amounts of phlox and yellow daisies line the trail and Mount Adams teases you with glimpses as you ascend. After 1.9 miles you will reach a sandy flat where the views – and the climbing – begin. Just 0.3 mile later, cross a small side creek in a beautiful meadow and then traverse another lovely meadow before crossing a creeklet. Continue climbing for another 0.5 mile, reaching a crossing of Crofton Creek in a deep, u-shaped gully. In November 2006, record-breaking rains obliterated this canyon. The creek crossing here is shockingly easy, despite the canyon's erosion. From here climb a steep and rocky 0.2 mile to a junction with the Round the Mountain Trail. Turn left.

The next 2.5 miles of level hiking are a feast of the senses. Wildflowers crowd the trail while Mount Adams looms larger than life to your right. Make your way through fields of volcanic rock, crossing Salt and Cascade Creeks in gullies lined with pink monkeyflower. Eventually you will enter a lovely hemlock forest and begin a light descent. At 2.4 miles from the Shorthorn Trail junction cross a creek with strange red rocks and shortly afterwards reach a junction with the Lookingglass Lake spur trail. Turn left again. Descend through forest and meadows on a rough trail. Along the way you will cross the red-rocked creek again, then several other smaller streams; if you aren't sure of the trail, look for flagging and follow the most obvious trail downhill. Keep straight at a junction and begin descending steeply, reaching the lake 1 mile from the Round the Mountain junction. Hike around the right side of the lake for views of Mount Adams. The turquoise waters and reflection of Mount Adams invite contemplation and the numerous excellent campsites in the area beckon to be occupied. Mosquitoes can be a problem in July, but will you really mind that much? You have paradise at your feet! Return the way you came or arrange a shuttle via the Stagman Ridge Trail (see below).

Other hiking options:
Lookingglass Lake via Stagman Ridge: You can also reach Lookingglass Lake on a shorter but less-scenic approach via Stagman Ridge. The Stagman Ridge Trail starts in the forest and climbs at a moderate grade for 3.5 miles to a junction with the Pacific Crest Trail. Turn right and hike 1.5 miles to the junction with the Lookingglass Lake spur trail. Follow this down to the lake, as noted above. When you wish to return, hike back up to a T-junction about 0.2 mile above the lake and turn left. Cross the red-rocked creek and continue hiking through gorgeous meadows on well-defined but seldom-used tread for 1 mile back to the Stagman Ridge Trail. Total distance: 10.7 miles with 2,400 feet of elevation gain. For directions consult the Portland Hikers Field Guide at the following link: http://bit.ly/UM4M1f

Trout Lake Big Tree: Though not exactly a hike, it is well worth a stop on the way to or from the Shorthorn Trailhead to see the Trout Lake Big Tree, a massive Ponderosa pine. At 84 inches in diameter and 202 feet tall, this giant is one of the largest remaining Ponderosa pines in the Gifford Pinchot National Forest. To find the Big Tree, drive 2.8 miles from the fork on FR 80 to a sign marked "Big Tree". If you are coming on the way back, this turn off is 0.9 mile after turning onto paved FR 80. Drive a potholed gravel road 0.2 mile to the Big Tree wayside and park. The tree is just off the road, behind the sign.

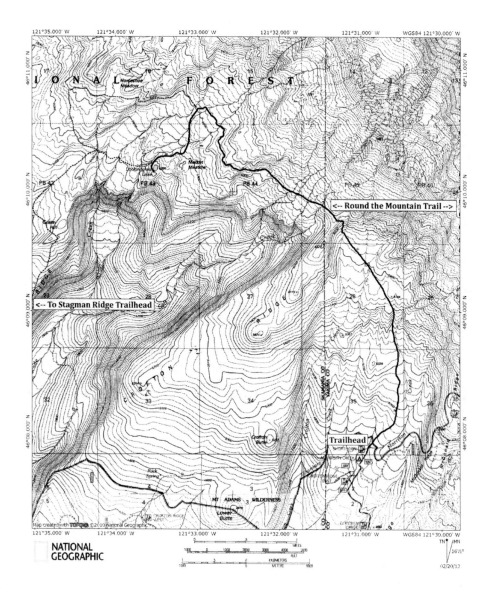

I O N A L   F O R E S T

Horseshoe Meadow

Madcat Meadow

<-- Round the Mountain Trail -->

<-- To Stagman Ridge Trailhead

Green

Creek

Creek

RIDGE

27

C R O F T O N

33

34

35

Crofton Butte

Trailhead

Rock Spring

MT ADAMS   WILDERNESS

Lower Butte

CROFTON RIDGE WEST

Map created with TOPO!® ©2010 National Geographic

MILES

FEET

KILOMETERS

METERS

TN / MN

16½°

02/20/13

47

Columbia River Gorge

16. Rock of Ages Ridge

Distance: 10.0 mile loop
Elevation Gain: 3,100 feet
Season: March – November
Best: June – July
Pass: None
Map: Columbia River Gorge (Geo-graphics)
Note: Rock of Ages Trail does not show on most area maps.

Directions: From Portland, drive east on Interstate 84 to the Bridal Veil exit 28. Immediately after exiting the freeway turn left and drive east on the Historic Columbia Highway 5.6 miles to a parking lot at Horsetail Falls. If you are coming from Cascade Locks, exit the freeway at the Dodson Exit 35 and drive west on the Historic Highway for 2.4 miles to Horsetail Falls.

Hike: A natural rock arch, a fabulous view of the Columbia River Gorge, a hair-raising rock spine, a serene forest high in the Gorge, a potentially challenging creek crossing and three waterfalls on a popular return trail; you will find all of these things on the trek up Rock of Ages Ridge and down Oneonta Creek. Though access is easy, the hike is not. In fact, the first mile up Rock of Ages Ridge is quite probably the most difficult stretch of trail in this book. After that, however, you are in the clear and free to enjoy the quietest part of the western Gorge.

The hike begins at scenic Horsetail Falls, which spills some 214 feet to the floor of the Gorge directly beside the scenic highway. The trailhead is to the left side of the falls. Begin switchbacking uphill, quickly topping out above the falls. Directly ahead of you on the trail is another falls, 75-foot Ponytail Falls. As soon as the falls is in sight, look immediately to your left for a well-worn boot path that climbs over some tree roots. This is the Rock of Ages Trail. Twenty yards from the turnoff pass a "Trail Not Maintained" sign – your cue that you are going to have some serious fun – and begin climbing at a furious pace. Because of the grade of this trail – and it is **brutally** steep – it is recommended that you avoid this trail on rainy days and that you avoid coming down this way (think bobsled run – but even more dangerous). After 0.5 mile of thigh-burning ascent, look for a spur trail to your right where the trail breaks back left; take this up and down path for 200 feet to a small natural rock arch and a spectacular view east over the Gorge. Even though you have only hiked 0.8 mile, you would be wise to break here as you have yet steeper uphill to go.

Return to the main trail and recommence climbing at the same unrelenting grade. You will likely need to use your hands (watch out for poison oak) and trekking poles are a must here. 0.3 mile from the arch the trail tops out at the Devil's Backbone, a frightening spine of rock with a 180 degree view of the Gorge. Acrophobes be warned! You can escape the worst of the Backbone by following a user trail to the left (and in fact, the trail more or less directs you this way now) but it is still recommended you spend a couple minutes checking out

the view here. Be **VERY** careful, though; a fall here would be serious. From here, begin climbing again through scenic second-growth forest for 1.7 miles (gaining another 1900 feet) to a junction with the Horsetail Creek trail 2.9 miles from the trailhead. Turn right.

The next 4 miles are a breeze after what you've endured. Meander through peaceful second-growth fir and pine at a mostly level grade, descending slightly to cross Horsetail Creek's three forks before ascending again. Without an official trailhead and high on a forested ridge, this is one of the quietest places in the Columbia River Gorge accessible by trail. Take the time to enjoy the silence – you have earned it.

About 3 miles from the Rock of Ages / Horsetail Creek trail junction, begin descending steadily towards Oneonta Creek via a series of switchbacks. Finally reach the creek 6.6 miles from the beginning of your hike and begin planning. In the summer this ford will not be difficult but in fall, winter and spring it is extremely challenging. Somebody has blazed a cutoff trail to the left that leads to the Oneonta Trail near a bridged crossing of the creek. While this trail appeared after I last hiked this trail, I strongly urge you to look for this trail and use it if possible (especially during the rainy season). However you choose to cross the creek, you will meet the Oneonta Trail almost immediately on the far side of the creek. There is a fantastic campsite at the junction of the Horsetail Creek Trail and Oneonta Trails.

From here the remainder of the hike is a cakewalk; an extremely popular, highly scenic cakewalk. Descend the well-maintained trail aside roaring Oneonta Creek. 1.5 miles later reach dazzling Triple Falls, a three-pronged 64-foot plunge. Continue another 0.5 mile downstream to a fork with the Horsetail Falls Trail. Turn right and descend to a breathtaking bridge over Oneonta Creek between its Middle Falls and the Lower Falls, out of sight below. Ascend quickly back up the canyon wall and follow this wide trail back to Ponytail Falls (the trail actually ducks behind the falls) and shortly thereafter, your car.

Other Hiking Options:
Oneonta Gorge: On a hot day in the summer (and only in the summer), if you still have some energy left this side trip is highly recommended. Drive (or walk) back on the Scenic Highway for a quarter mile to the pullout for Oneonta Gorge. Wade upstream from here a quarter-mile (traversing an epic logjam along the way) to Lower Oneonta Falls, tucked away in a slot canyon so narrow fallen trees form bridges over it. If you've come here on a summer weekend you will have to fight the masses – this is one of the holiest of sanctuaries in the Columbia River Gorge. If you want the place to yourself, aim for a weekday morning.

Wauneka Point via Rock of Ages: If you turn left at the Rock of Ages – Horsetail Creek junction instead of right, you will hike 2.6 miles to road near Nesmith Point described in Hike 17. Turn right and hike 0.1 mile to find the Moffett Creek Trail, where you then hike toward Wauneka Point. This approach is only slightly longer than what is described in Hike 17, is much quieter and is perhaps more scenic.

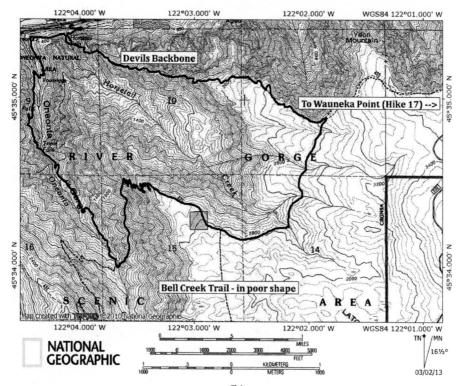

17. Wauneka Point

Distance: 17.2 miles
Elevation Gain: 4,400 feet
Season: June – November
Best: July – October
Pass: None.
Map: Columbia River Gorge (Geo-graphics)

Directions: From Portland, drive east on Interstate 84 to exit 35, signed for Ainsworth State Park and the Columbia River Historic Highway. Turn left at a fork and then arrive at a junction with Frontage Road, signed for Dodson and Warrendale. Turn left at this junction and drive 2.2 miles to road's end at the signed trailhead for John B. Yeon State Park.

Hike: Of all the special places in the Gorge, Wauneka Point may be the most special of all. The point is a wide, rocky outcrop that features many Indian pits and mysterious rock formations; the view looks down the Gorge for miles in each direction, with the volcanoes of Southwest Washington looming above the Gorge walls. If that was difficult to imagine, then you need to hike to Wauneka Point to see for yourself. There is only one catch: the hike is extremely difficult and extremely long, and is probably best served as a backpacking trip. It is absolutely worth the effort.

Begin by hiking on the Elowah Falls Trail. After just 500 feet, reach a trail junction with the Nesmith Point Trail. Turn right here and begin a moderate climb through attractive forest. Before long, the climb becomes quite steep in true Gorge fashion with long, steep and frequent switchbacks. The way becomes somewhat less steep after 2 miles but continues to climb as it traverses a rocky, sometimes-open slope. You will re-enter the forest as you continue to switchback up, following a narrow box canyon full of large cedar trees. After about 4 miles, the trail begins to level out at the Gorge rim and traverses over to a junction with a long-abandoned road to the summit of Nesmith Point at 4.6 miles. While Nesmith Point is close at hand (there is a spur just 500 feet down the abandoned road that leads to the summit), the views are obstructed.

Hiking on the old road, pass the Nesmith Point Spur in 0.1 mile, a junction with the Horsetail Creek Trail after another 0.1 mile and reach a signed junction with the Moffett Creek Trail at 0.3 mile from the end of the Nesmith Point Trail. Turn left on the Moffett Creek Trail and begin descending gradually. When you bottom out, you will cross the first of two forks of McCord Creek in verdant, mossy forest. A short trail leads to a great campsite just feet from a marshy lake. If you are camping, this makes for a great stopping point. Past the campsite and the lake the trail begins a moderate climb, crosses the second fork of McCord Creek and climbs again to a signed junction with the Wauneka Point Trail at 1.7 miles from the abandoned road and 6.6 miles from the trailhead. Turn left.

The Wauneka Point Trail follows a narrow ridge back to the north towards the Columbia River. As you hike down the ridge, the trail becomes increasingly faint; while it never quite disappears, it requires careful attention in places to avoid losing it. About 1.5 miles from the junction, you will reach a rockslide with a cairn. Traverse down the rockslide to locate the continuation of the trail. From here, the trail descends slightly until you reach Wauneka Point at 8.6 miles from the trailhead. As mentioned earlier, the view is astounding. Even more fascinating are the Indian pits. It is believed that young Indians used such sites in their vision quests, when they would fast and commune with nature for several days until they received a vision of their future and their role in the world. In any case, the rock formations and pits at Wauneka Point are extremely fragile – please try to avoid damaging them in your explorations at the point.

Return the way you came.

Other Hiking Options:
Wauneka / Tanner Loop: Backpackers or extremely fit day hikers can combine the trip to Wauneka Point with a hike down the Tanner Creek Road to the Wahclella Falls Trailhead.

To make the loop, instead of returning the way you came after visiting Wauneka Point, continue straight on the Moffett Creek Trail (here you would turn left on the Moffett Creek Trail to continue the loop rather than turn right to return to your car at the Nesmith Point Trailhead) past a series of ponds until the trail begins an extremely steep descent into Tanner Creek's canyon nearly 3 miles from the Wauneka Trail junction. Ford wide and swift Tanner Creek, and shortly after reach the Tanner Creek Trail. Turn left on the trail and reach abandoned

Tanner Creek Road after 1.3 miles. Follow this road for 3.5 mostly-level miles to a junction with the Gorge Trail. Turn left here and hike 0.7 miles to the Wahclella Falls Trail and another 3 miles back to the Yeon Trailhead to complete the loop, passing under beautiful Elowah Falls near the end. The total distance of this hike is 22 miles with approximately 4,500 feet of elevation gain.

Alternately, you can arrange a short car shuttle to the Wahclella Falls Trailhead, shaving three miles off the round-trip distance of the loop. To find the Wahclella Falls Trailhead, drive east on Interstate 84 another 5 miles east past the Dodson Exit to Exit 40, signed for Bonneville Dam. At the bottom of the off ramp, turn right and drive into the Wahclella Falls Trailhead (NW Forest Pass required).

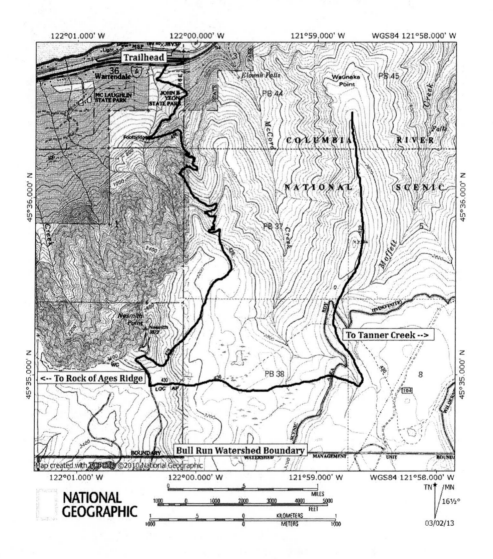

18. Ruckel Ridge

Distance: 9.6 mile loop
Elevation Gain: 3,800 feet
Season: May – November
Best: May – June
Trailhead Pass: NW Forest Pass
Map: Columbia River Gorge (Geo-Graphics)
Note: Ruckel Ridge Trail does not show on this map.

Directions: Drive Interstate 84 east of Portland to Eagle Creek Exit 41. Almost immediately after exiting the freeway, you park in a lot on the left next to a fish hatchery. As this lot also doubles as a parking lot for the very busy Eagle Creek Trail, it is recommended that you arrive early on sunny spring and summer days. Leave nothing of value in your car as break-ins and clouting are frequent occurrences in this part of the Gorge.

Hike: The Ruckel Ridge loop is one of the most difficult hikes in this book. This steep, rugged circuit will leave you gasping for breath and hoping you didn't brush against some of the ubiquitous poison oak along the trail. This loop, however, is also some of the most fun you will ever have on a trail and ranks as one of my favorites in the Columbia River Gorge. Come prepared for a long day of incredibly steep trails, some exposure, a lot of poison oak and a knee-jarring descent that will leave your joints aching for days. Thankfully, you'll conveniently overlook all of this until your return. This is *the* legendary lost trail in the Columbia River Gorge.

The hike begins in the overcrowded lower Eagle Creek parking lot. Follow a paved road 0.3 mile to the similarly overcrowded and noisy Eagle Creek campground. Hike through the campground to campsite #5, following signs for the Buck Point Trail. Turn right here, escape the din of both campground and interstate and begin switchbacking steeply up to Buck Point, an open spot under powerlines with a nice view of Mount Adams. Take a breather here and perhaps remove a layer as well. It gets **much** steeper from here on out.

Pass a "Trail Not Maintained" sign, drop a bit and then begin traversing up an extremely steep slope towards a ridge that looks impossible to reach. You'll need your hands here as you zigzag around the first citadels of Ruckel Ridge. From here the trail reenters the forest and begins a rollercoaster of short downs and very long ups. Note the basalt pillars that make up the crest of the ridge-you'll be climbing around and over them for most of the ascent. It is here that the poison oak is most prevalent, so keep your eyes peeled!

After 2 miles and 2,700 feet of merciless climbing you come to a section affectionately known as the Catwalk. Here the trail follows the narrow crest of the ridge as it dwindles down to a two-foot wide knife-edge with steep drop-offs on each side. Acrophobes may choose an alternate route that skirts the Catwalk on the bottom right, but for those who want to live on the edge simply follow the knife-edge to where it culminates in the only technical move of the hike, a reverse two-step on an 18-inch wide section of exposed rock. Though less than 0.1 mile, the Catwalk is frightening enough to get adrenaline pumping through even the hardiest hikers.

After taking a well-earned breather, continue climbing through a forest of spindly pines. About halfway into the summit push at an elevation of approximately 3,200 feet, follow a short side trail to your right out to a stupendous view of the upper Eagle Creek valley with Mount Hood looming over the lip of the canyon. Take a minute to soak up the view before you continue. Back on the trail, switchback up steeply another 600 feet of elevation until the trail abruptly levels off atop the Benson Plateau. Here the trail more or less disappears. Turn left and follow both cut trees and orange tree blazes across the densely forested plateau approximately half a mile to a crossing of Ruckel Creek. For most of the year the creek is a mere trickle but early in the season it may be difficult to cross with dry feet. Once across the creek follow blazes down a bit to a junction with the well-signed and well-maintained Ruckel Creek Trail at 4.8 miles. Turn left.

As steep as your ascent up Ruckel Ridge was, the descent down the Ruckel Creek Trail is somehow even steeper. One of the steepest trails in an area full of steep trails, the Ruckel Creek Trail will crunch your knees and jam your toes as you seemingly take flight from the Benson Plateau. Trekking poles are highly recommended. Thankfully, there are some scenic highlights during the trip down that help break up the monotony of the knee-crunching, ankle-turning descent. Approximately 0.75 down the trail follow the sound of falling water left at a switchback to a beautiful cascade on Ruckel Creek. Further down the trail, traverse a series of hanging meadows at about 2,300 feet of elevation. In May and early June look for yellow violets, pink shooting stars, larkspur, paintbrush and the elusive brown Chocolate lily. Continue switchbacking down and down and down...and down. At approximately 1,000 feet of elevation you'll hike by a

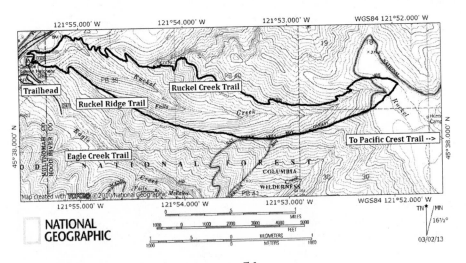

talus slope. The pits you see scattered here are the remains of Indian vision quest sites; do not disturb them! Rejoice, as your descent is almost done. From here drop down steeply to the old Columbia River Highway just above Lower Ruckel Falls. It is possible to bushwhack down to the base of this lovely cascade but you'll probably just be bushed. Turn left and follow the old road, now-closed to cars, half a mile to your car.

19. Dry Creek Falls via Herman Creek

Distance: 8.0 miles out and back
Elevation Gain: 1,000 feet
Season: All year
Best: April – May
Trailhead Pass: NW Forest Pass
Map: Columbia River Gorge [Geo-graphics]

Directions: Drive Interstate 84 East from Portland to exit 44 for Cascade Locks. Drive through town, east, and then pass under the freeway at the far end of town. Continue straight and east on Frontage Road. After 2 miles you will come to a sign for Herman Creek Campground. In the winter you need to park here as the road is gated; otherwise, drive up the campground road to the trailhead.

Hike: Dry Creek Falls is one of the quietest waterfalls in the Columbia River Gorge accessible by trail. Most people who hike to the falls arrive via perhaps the dullest stretch of the Pacific Crest Trail in the state of Oregon, beginning in Cascade Locks at a parking lot at the Bridge of the Gods. While this access is certainly convenient at only 2.2 miles from the falls, there is another, far more interesting way to get to Dry Creek Falls: via Herman Creek and a PCT connector trail. Along the way you'll cross a fantastic bridge over Herman Creek, pass some fascinating rock pinnacles, cross a talus slope with views across the Columbia River to Table Mountain and check out a bonus waterfall deep in a rock cleft. Even though the hike is twice as long as the westerly approach, it is at least twice as interesting.

The hike begins at the Herman Creek Campground. In winter the gate to the campground may be locked, necessitating a walk up the approach road, adding another 0.4 mile to your hike. From the trailhead set off uphill on a section of trail that is very muddy in winter. Quickly cross under the powerlines and continue to a junction with the Herman Bridge trail 406E at 0.6 mile. Turn right and switchback downhill through attractive forest to a metal bridge over Herman Creek, a raging torrent in winter months. Take a few moments to linger at the bridge and then continue uphill on the opposite side, climbing out of the canyon on a steady incline. You'll gain most of the hike's elevation gain in this mile-long section. At 2.0 miles from your car, intersect the PCT at a poorly-marked junction.

Turn right here and immediately traverse a massive talus slope where you will likely hear the *meep!* of the pika in summer months. Shortly thereafter reach Pacific Crest Falls on your left, set in a lovely rock cleft above the trail. It is possible to bushwhack to the base of the falls but watch your footing! The rocks below the falls are not stable and very slick. Just a few hundred yards past the falls you come to a series of strange rock pinnacles. There are trails circling the formations but scaling them is not recommended to hikers without climbing experience.

From the pinnacles the trail traverses another massive talus slope, this one with views across Cascade Locks and the Columbia River to Table Mountain. Twisted oaks frame the scene. Listen for the roar of the interstate below; this is the only time you will hear it along the course of this hike. Continue west and re-enter the forest, passing through attractive woods with some old-growth mixed in. After a bit look down to your right at a fern-covered depression in the forest; you are getting close now! Cross a bridge over Dry Creek at 4.0 miles from your car and come to a road on the opposite side. Turn left and hike 0.2 mile up to Dry Creek Falls, a 75-foot plunge in an impressive basalt amphitheater. Take a moment to inspect the machinery and concrete works at the base-this is Cascade Locks' water source. Please be kind to this area.

Return the way you came or continue on the Pacific Crest Trail to Cascade Locks, a 6.6 mile hike. Unless you arranged a shuttle you will need to hike back either the trail or walk through Cascade Locks and along Frontage Road 3 miles to the Herman Creek Trailhead.

Other Hiking Options:

PCT to Benson Plateau: If you turn left at the junction of the Herman Bridge Trail and the Pacific Crest Trail instead of going straight to Dry Creek Falls, you will begin a long, gradual ascent up to the Benson Plateau (See Hike 18). While this section of the PCT is never spectacular, it is quite beautiful in its own right as it climbs through peaceful woods, passing a couple of nice viewpoints and Teakettle Spring before topping out on the Benson Plateau at a junction with Benson Way Trail, a total of 3.9 miles from the PCT – Herman Bridge trail junction. From here you can continue south, passing numerous trail junctions until you reach a junction with the Ruckel Creek Trail in another 1.4 miles. From there the way leads to Wahtum Lake (Hike 20) and eventually to Mexico. Although there are nicer hikes in the area, this hike is great if you want a lot of exercise without punishing your body the way other trails in this area do.

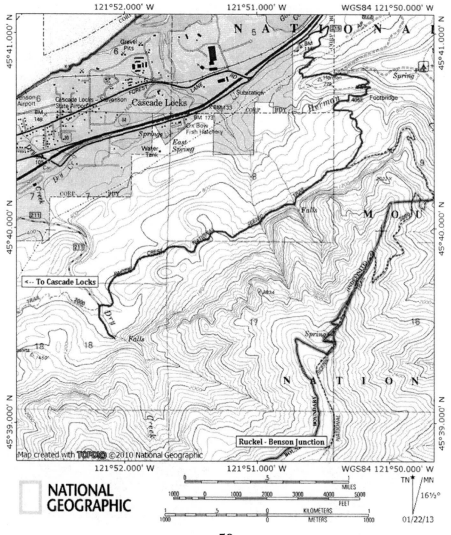

20. Indian Mountain

Distance: 8.6 miles out and back
Elevation Gain: 1,200 feet
Season: June – October
Best: July – August
Pass: NW Forest Pass
Map: Mount Hood Wilderness Map (Geo-Graphics)

Directions: From Portland, drive east on Interstate 84 to Hood River. At Exit 63, leave the interstate and turn right to drive into Hood River. Drive 2 blocks south (uphill) to Oak Street and turn right again. Drive 11 blocks west to a junction with 13th Street. Turn left here and drive uphill out of downtown Hood River on 13th Street, which soon becomes OR 281. After a little more than 5 miles on OR 281, keep right at a sign for Tucker Park to stay on OR 281. Continue 6.5 miles on OR 281 to a junction signed for Lost Lake. Turn right, cross the Hood River, and turn left at a junction that is also signed for Lost Lake. Stay on this road, following signs for Lost Lake at every junction, for almost 5 miles to a junction with FR 13 just after you enter the Mount Hood National Forest. Turn right on FR 13 at a sign for Wahtum Lake and drive 4.3 miles to another junction. Keep to the right for another 6 miles to the Wahtum Lake Trailhead on your right.

Hike: Situated at the head of Eagle Creek's famed valley, Wahtum Lake has long been a favored destination for backpackers and PCT through-hikers. Few hikers rarely take the time to explore this beautiful area. Even fewer hikers are aware of perhaps the area's best viewpoints, on the open slopes and summit of Indian Mountain. Best of all, the hike is quite easy, as you let your vehicle do all the work. It almost feels like cheating!

Begin at the Wahtum Lake trailhead, which is also a small campground. At the signboard, hike straight and downhill on the Wahtum Express Trail. This path

quickly drops to the lakeshore via more than 250 steps. Reach a junction with the Pacific Crest Trail near the shore. Turn left. You will hike around deep, scenic Wahtum Lake almost 0.5 mile to another trail junction, this one with the Eagle Creek Trail. Keep left and leave the lake to begin a long, gentle ascent through verdant, old-growth forest. At 2.3 miles from the trailhead, leave the forest as you parallel FR 660, a seldom-used gravel road that connects Wahtum Lake and an upper trailhead for Indian Mountain (see **Other Hiking Options**). As you pass directly above this road, a fabulous view of Mount Hood to the south enchants hikers. Stay on the trail and descend gently to primitive and seldom-used Indian Springs Campground at 3.2 miles from the trailhead.

Continue straight on the PCT, crossing the campground access road and passing two signboards. You will curve around the lower slopes of Indian Mountain to a junction with the Indian Mountain Trail 3.7 miles from the trailhead. The view here is stupendous: while Mount Saint Helens, Mount Rainier and Mount Adams loom on the horizon, the real star here is the 180 degree view of the upper Columbia River Gorge. Veteran Gorge hikers will be able to pick out Larch Mountain, Silver Star Mountain, Table Mountain, Chinidere Mountain and Mount Defiance (to the northeast – look for the radio towers). Immediately to your left is hulking Tanner Butte, while the entirety of Eagle Creek's long canyon spreads out beneath you. As good as this is, don't turn around yet! Turn left at the cairn onto the Indian Mountain Trail. You will ascend open slopes where the trail is a bit vague (follow the huge cairns) to the remains of a summit access road. Follow this road into the forest as it becomes a trail. You will stay in the forest until you switchback up to the summit of Indian Mountain at 4.3 miles. A former lookout site (watch for broken glass and nails on the ground, as well as the remains of an outhouse just below the summit), the view to the south is outstanding. Mount Hood appears surprisingly close over the upper Hood River valley, while Mount Jefferson, Three-Fingered Jack and everything in between are visible on the southern horizon. The concrete foundations of the old lookout tower make great seats for lunch. Return the way you came.

Other Hiking Options:
Indian Mountain Road: As noted above, you can drive to the Indian Springs Campground and turn an 8.6 mile hike into a 2.6 mile hike. As of this writing, the road (FR 660) is in great shape and is easily manageable for any passenger vehicle. To drive to this upper trailhead, continue past the Wahtum Lake Trailhead for 3 gravel miles on FR 660 to an unsigned junction with the Indian Springs Campground access road. Turn right and drive 100 yards to the campground and trailhead. The road was recently rebuilt but does not receive frequent maintenance.

Scout Lake: This small lake just a half-mile south of Wahtum Lake receives very little use and makes for a nice side trip after hiking to Indian Mountain. To find Scout Lake, drive south past the Wahtum Lake Trailhead 0.5 mile to an unsigned road junction with FR 661. Turn left and drive 100 yards to a pullout on the left. Look for a brushy trail heading steeply downhill to your left (there is also a blank signboard on a tree above the trail). This trail drops quickly to a poor campsite above the lake. Turn right and traverse around the south side of the lake to the brushy lakeshore. Though abandoned, somebody has maintained this trail recently and the tread is rarely difficult to follow.

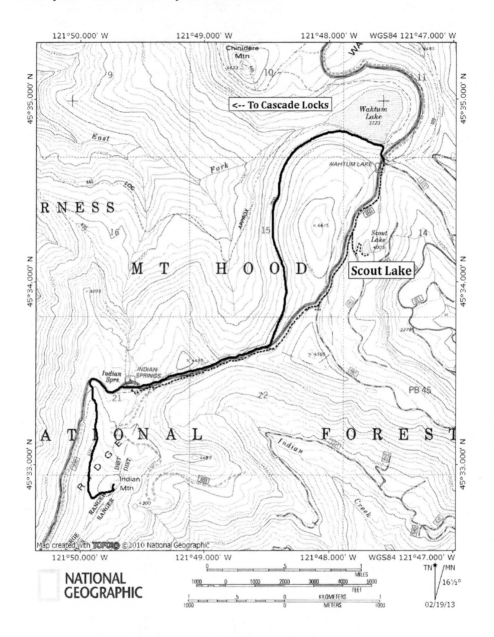

21. Bald Butte

Distance: 8.4 miles out and back
Elevation Gain: 2400 feet
Season: April – November
Best: April – June
Pass: None
Map: None needed.

Directions: From Portland, drive Interstate 84 to Hood River and leave the highway at Exit 64, signed for OR 35 and Mount Hood. Drive south 14.4 miles on this paved, 2-lane highway. Just past Tollbridge County Park, turn left on Smullen Road at a sign for the Oak Ridge Trail. Drive 0.25 mile to another sign and turn left on a gravel road into the trailhead.

Hike: Very similar in character to famed Dog Mountain in the Columbia River Gorge, the trail to Bald Butte climbs up gorgeous open meadows to a windy summit with spectacular wildflower displays in May and June. What separates these two hikes, however, are two things: first, the trail to Bald Butte trades views of the Columbia River Gorge (one of Dog Mountain's famed attributes) for stunning views of Mount Hood looming over the upper Hood River Valley as well as views out to Mounts Saint Helens, Adams and Rainier; second, aside from a short stretch of trail that is popular with mountain bikers, you won't see even a fraction of the amount of people you would see on Dog Mountain.

Begin by hiking up the Oak Ridge Trail. Skirt a clearcut where you will be compensated with outstanding views across to Mount Hood and, in season, a large variety of flowers such as wild rose and bachelor button. Enter a pleasant forest dominated by Douglas fir and the occasional Ponderosa pine and begin climbing. Before too long you will leave the forest and begin a gradual traverse up an open, grassy slope with fantastic views of the Mount Hood and the upper Hood River Valley. In addition to the views, the wildflowers are superb. Look for the usual suspects (balsamroot, lupine and paintbrush) as well as more bachelor button and the occasional wild onion. Mount Hood looms supreme over the Hood River Valley. If you can pull yourself away, keep climbing and reenter the forest at 1.5 miles from the trailhead. Here the grade relents somewhat and you are rewarded with the occasional view out to Bald Butte (which appears much further away than it actually is) and copious amounts of small pink calypso orchids in May and June. At 2.3 miles the trail crosses a closed logging road and just a few hundred yards later, ends at a junction with the Surveyor's Ridge Trail. Turn left.

The next mile of trail is mostly open, passing through meadows and recovering clearcuts with nice views out to Mount Hood and ahead to Mount Adams. Pay attention here, as the Surveyor's Ridge Trail is very popular with mountain bikers (and justifiably so). Before too long you will lose a bit of elevation and reach the end of the trail at a well-signed trailhead, complete with picnic table. Ahead of you is the double-humped summit of Bald Butte. Follow an old jeep road under powerlines to the first summit. Here reenter the forest, lose a bit of elevation and quickly emerge below the second, true summit. Here the road steepens considerably amid hanging meadows. Arrive shortly at the summit meadows and soak up the scenery; in addition to the impressive flower displays, the views are truly jaw-dropping on a clear day, extending the entire length of the Hood River Valley. Look to your left (southwest) to Mount Hood, guarded on the east by bulky Lookout Mountain in the Badger Creek Wilderness. Look to your right (north) to Hood River, with Mounts Saint Helens and Rainier looming over the Cascades of the Gifford Pinchot. Despite near-constant winds this is a superb picnic spot. When you can force yourself to leave, return the way you came.

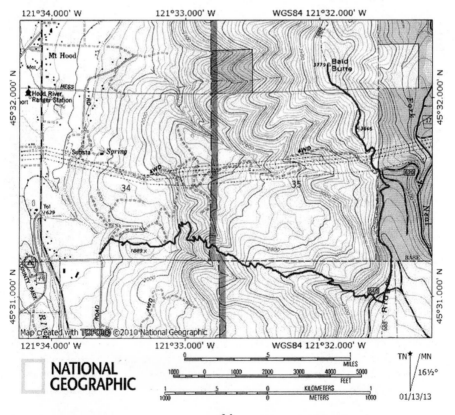

22. Stacker Butte

Distance: 4.8 miles
Elevation Gain: 1,300 feet
Season: March – November
Best: April – May
Trailhead Pass: Washington Discovery Pass ($10)
Map: None needed.

Directions: From Portland drive east on Interstate 84 for 80 miles to The Dalles. At a sign for US 197 at Exit 87, leave the freeway. Turn left and cross the Columbia River. Continue on this highway for 2 more miles to a junction with WA 14. Turn right and in just 1 mile, turn left on the Dalles Mountain Road at a sign for Marshal's Winery. Continue straight on this road past a junction for the winery and continue 3.3 miles to a junction at a barn. For a longer hike, park at the barn and walk the rest of the road. Otherwise, turn a sharp left and drive up the rutted, narrow gravel road another 1.4 miles to a small parking lot at a locked gate. The hike description begins at the locked gate.

Hike: While many come to the open fields at the Dalles Mountain Ranch during wildflower season in May, few bother to hike the road all the way to the top of Stacker Butte. Their loss. From the top of the butte at the end of the road the view is jaw-dropping, stretching from the Three Sisters all the way to Mount Rainier as well as forty miles of the Columbia River Gorge. Come here on a sunny day in May and you'll see a few parties hiking with you to the top. If wildflowers aren't your bag, come here in the fall or winter and you'll likely be all alone. Avoid this hike in July and August when this part of the Gorge roasts in 100º heat.

Begin at the gated road. In season the wildflower show is among the best in the Gorge, featuring the usual showstoppers balsamroot and lupine. Also keep a lookout for white Hood's phlox, yellow buttercups and pink clover. The road winds up the treeless slopes of Stacker Butte. Keen eyes may spot deer or coyotes on the slopes above and across from you while birds serenade you. Mount Hood looms larger than life across the Columbia River.

1.8 miles from the road gate, pass a radio tower and maintenance building on your right. The top of Stacker Butte is now ahead of you. Hike the last 0.6 mile to the top of the butte with its collection of radio transmitters. Among these is fenced-off facility managed by the Federal Aviation Administration – so don't trespass. While the collection of towers and radio equipment might detract a bit from the scene, what will grab your attention is the view. Oh, what a view it is! Mount Adams and Mount Rainier and the Goat Rocks tower over the surrounding farmland to your north while Mount Hood seems to guard The Dalles to the south. Further south is glaciated Mount Jefferson. On clear days you can see the Three Sisters to the left of Mount Jefferson. The Gorge to the south and Swale Canyon (Hike 23) to the north are at your feet. Views rarely get better than this anywhere in the Pacific Northwest. When you've had enough (or you've had enough of the near constant winds), return the way you came.

Other Hiking Options:
Eightmile Creek Falls: Either before or after you hike up to Stacker Butte, this beautiful desert waterfall is worth visiting. Continue east past Dalles Mountain Road on WA 14 another 2.7 miles, passing Horsethief Butte, to a metal gate at milepost 87. The best place to park is at the gate on the left side of the road. The falls is visible from the road but for a better view, hike up this old road 0.4 mile to an overlook immediately above the falls. The old road, now a trail, continues another 0.5 mile up Eightmile Creek to a fence with a view up to Stacker Butte. It is possible to continue towards Stacker Butte from here but access is sketchy – there are fences everywhere. You should instead return the way you came.

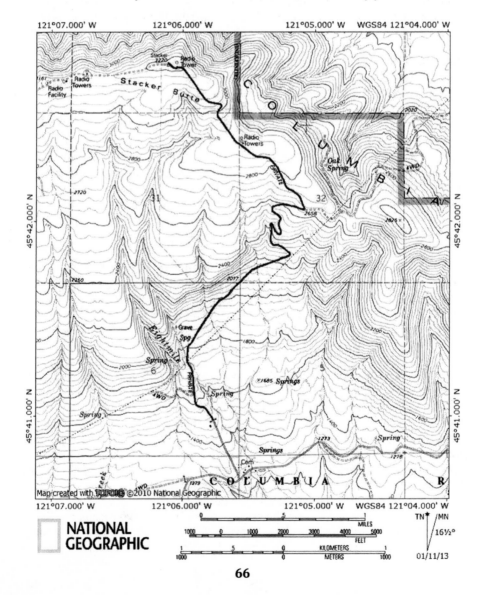

23. Swale Canyon

Distance: 10.2 miles out and back
Elevation Gain: 450 feet
Season: October – June
Best: March – May
Pass: None needed.
Map: None needed.
Note: Closed in summer due to fire danger.

Directions: From Portland drive east on Interstate 84 to Hood River. Following signs for OR 35, leave the freeway at Exit 64 and turn left at the end of the off ramp. Immediately arrive at the bridge over the Columbia River. Pay the $1 toll and cross the narrow bridge. On the other side of the river at a junction turn right and drive 11 miles to the town of Lyle. In the center of town turn left on the Centerville Highway and drive this two-lane paved road 14.7 miles through the country to a junction with Harms Road. Turn left here and drive this gravel road 0.5 mile to a marked trailhead where the old Klickitat Railway crossed the road. There is room for a few cars on the trailhead side of the road.

Hike: Similar to the nearby Deschutes River Trail (Hike 24), the trip down Swale Canyon is a wonderful slice of semi-desert scenery on a converted railway just two hours from Portland. Here, however, you will see even fewer people and even more wildlife, making for a perfect getaway. If you come in the winter you stand a decent chance of staying dry and a great chance of being completely alone out here. Sound like fun? It should.

From the remote upper trailhead set off downstream on the converted rail trail through a pastoral setting of farmlands. Looming above you on your left is Stacker Butte (Hike 22). Swale Creek is but a trickle here. Round a bend and begin descending into the canyon. From here on out keep your eyes and ears peeled – in this open terrain you have an excellent chance of spotting all kinds of wildlife from snakes to marmots to deer. Given the open, grassy terrain it is also advised you keep an eye out for ticks in the springtime.

Slowly the canyon reveals itself to you, step by step. The canyon walls grow taller, and the arid farm country of the trailhead gives way to basalt rock formations on the canyon wall, scattered pine trees and copious wildflowers that last from March to June. Cross Swale Creek again and again on low trestles, all that remains of the railway that used to cut through this canyon. The scenery is consistently great, making it more and more difficult to turn around. Unless you have arranged a time-consuming car shuttle, you will eventually need to turn around; where you choose to do so is up to you. Swale Creek bends to the north at 4.5 miles from the trailhead, and 0.6 mile later reach a series of small bedrock pools on the creek. This is a great spot from which to turn around; though the scenery is excellent downstream as well, this is perhaps the loveliest spot in all of Swale Canyon. Return the way you came; to set up a car shuttle at the bottom of Swale Canyon, see below.

Other Hiking Options:
If you would prefer to hike the whole of Swale Canyon you must establish a car shuttle, leaving a car at the lower trailhead near the small town of Wahkiakus. To reach this lower trailhead, drive to Lyle as described above and turn left (north) on WA 142. Drive 16.2 miles to the small town of Wahkiakus and turn right on Horseshoe Bend Road. Cross the Klickitat River and turn into a parking lot signed for the Klickitat River Trail. To connect to the upper trailhead from here, continue on gravel Horseshoe Bend for 4.9 miles to a junction with Harms Road. Continue straight on gravel Harms Road for 3.5 miles to the upper trailhead listed above. Establishing the shuttle will take you the better part of an hour so prepare accordingly. You will pass several houses on the lower part of Swale Canyon before exiting the canyon. The terrain is still beautiful, but much less scenic than the upper part of the canyon.

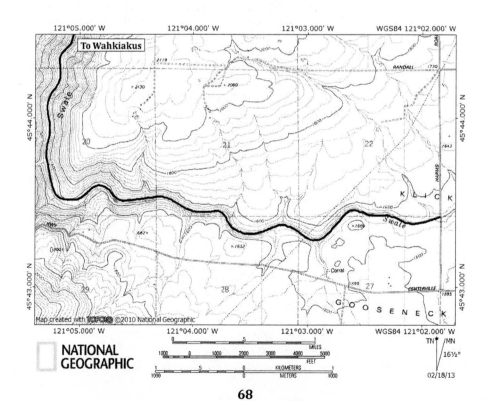

24. Deschutes River Trail

Distance: 11.2 miles out and back
Elevation Gain: 300 feet
Season: all year (avoid midsummer heat)
Best: April – May
Pass: State Park Fee
Map: Columbia River Gorge (Geo-graphics)

Directions: From Portland, drive 75 miles to The Dalles on Interstate 84 and continue another 13 miles to Exit 97. Following signs for the Deschutes Recreation Area, leave the freeway at Exit 97 and arrive at a junction. Turn left and drive 3 miles to Deschutes State Park. Cross the river and turn right into the campground. Drive through the campground and park at the south end of the B campground loop, near the camp host and bathrooms. The trail is straight ahead at the end of a grassy field.

Hike: Just 90 minutes from Portland, the transition from wet Western Oregon to dry, desert-like Eastern Oregon culminates at the mouth of the Deschutes River. Follow an old road and brushy trails up this gorgeous, nearly treeless canyon to a plethora of great campsites, abandoned boxcars and a weathered, century-old homestead. This does not feel like anywhere else you've visited in our corner of Oregon. Avoid this canyon in the summer when it bakes in 100º heat; this is often the hottest place in the state of Oregon.

The trail begins on the lawn at the end of the B-Loop in Deschutes State Park Campground. Look for a trail heading upstream that follows the river. Shortly you will reach a junction with a trail darting uphill; this is the way to the road and a possible return trail. Here you are presented with a dilemma; the trail ahead follows the river closely but is brushy and at times, poorly defined. To complicate matters further, this trail is known for its high population of ticks in spring. If you hate the little arachnids or are traveling with dogs, turn left and head uphill. Otherwise, head straight and follow the river as the trail weaves and bounces over rocks, past beaches and through tall sagebrush. The further you get upstream, the fainter the tread becomes. After 3 miles, come to the first campsite at Colorado Rapids, complete with a vault toilet. Here the user trail dies; instead follow the access road up to the road bed above. If you've arrived here by hiking the road and wish to visit this nice campsite, head downhill on the access road towards the bathroom. If you're camping, there are plenty of spaces to pitch a tent.

From here join the road as it climbs above the river next to an incredible basalt cliff. Notice how the rock has formed in numerous strange and phantasmagoric formations, among them a bizarre eye of radiating basalt emanating out of a cave about 30 feet above the road. The canyon here is stunning with basalt cliffs, green treeless slopes and, amazingly, what look like tide pools in the river below. The explorer will be tempted to climb up to the ridge top on any number of

extremely steep user trails but beware – the rock is crumbly. Be safe or be sorry. At 5.6 miles from the trailhead you will come to an abandoned wooden boxcar just off the trail to your right. This is one of the few reminders that your trail (well, actually a closed road) was once a railroad line along the Deschutes River. A better rest or lunch spot would be hard to imagine as the boxcar offers protection from the wind and sun and gives you a fantastic destination for your day hike.

Other Hiking Options:
Harris Homestead: Backpackers or extremely motivated hikers can continue another 5.3 miles upriver to an abandoned homestead that has become weathered with time. While nobody has lived here for quite a while, the farm here is still used from time to time. From this point you can continue upstream another 12 very scenic miles to an extremely remote upper trailhead at Mack's Canyon. The trail becomes rougher beyond Harris Homestead but is still reasonably easy to hike for the most part.

For directions to the upper trailhead, drive to White River Falls (Hike 34) and continue down to the falls at Sherar's Bridge on the Deschutes River. Cross a bridge over the Deschutes River and turn left (north) on a gravel road maintained by the Bureau of Land Management. You will drive this washboarded road 17 miles to the Mack's Canyon Trailhead at the end of the road. There is a small campground at this trailhead. For more information on this hike, consult the Portland Hikers Field Guide: http://bit.ly/XHxvoj

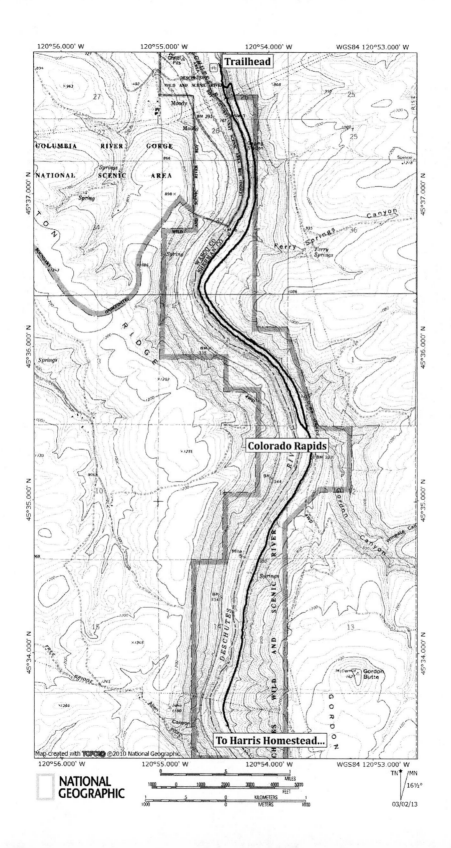

Trailhead

Colorado Rapids

To Harris Homestead...

120°56.000' W   120°55.000' W   120°54.000' W   WGS84 120°53.000' W

120°56.000' W   120°55.000' W   120°54.000' W   WGS84 120°53.000' W

45°37.000' N

45°36.000' N

45°35.000' N

45°34.000' N

COLUMBIA   RIVER   GORGE
NATIONAL   SCENIC   AREA

Map created with TOPO!® ©2010 National Geographic

NATIONAL
GEOGRAPHIC

TN   /MN
16½°

03/02/13

Mount Hood and Badger Creek

25. Horseshoe Ridge

Distance: 11 miles out and back
Elevation Gain: 2,700 feet
Season: June – October
Best: June – July
Pass: NW Forest Pass
Map: Mount Hood Wilderness Area (Geo-Graphics)

Directions: Drive east on US 26 for 35 miles to Zigzag and Rhododendron. At a stop light with a sign for East Lolo Pass Road (FR 18), turn left and follow the Sandy River north. Stay on Lolo Pass Road for 4 paved miles to a junction with FR 1825 that is labeled "campgrounds trailheads" and after 0.6 mile of paved road turn right to cross the Sandy River. Follow FR 1825 another 0.4 mile to a junction with FR 382. Turn right and immediately look for pullouts on both sides of the road. The signed trail departs to your right.

Hike: Trying to find a great viewpoint of the west side of Mount Hood without fighting the hordes is difficult. In hiking up to the fabulous viewpoint on Zigzag Ridge via the Horseshoe Ridge Trail, you can appreciate magnificent alpine splendor in almost virtual solitude. Furthermore, a 2007 road washout has lengthened the hike by 4 miles and added 700 more feet of elevation gain, virtually ensuring you'll be almost alone on this wonderful hike. Finally, you can add in a loop to a beautiful but seldom-visited lake to make a moderate overnight backpack or a long, difficult day hike. This is a hike that is not to be missed.

Begin just outside the Riley Horse Camp. Ignore signs for the Cast Creek Trail (this is your return route should you choose to make this a loop) and instead choose the Horseshoe Ridge Trail. Follow this trail for a sandy, flat mile to a crossing of Lost Creek in deep forest. Cross the creek on a long metal bridge and almost immediately begin climbing. Here it is time to strike up a conversation as you will be climbing for the rest of the way to your destination. After a mile of relatively gentle uphill from the bridge, reach the old trailhead at a pullout on a now-closed section of FR380. Look for the continuation of the trail across the old road and continue climbing, entering the Mount Hood Wilderness Area just after crossing the road.

On this switchbacking 3.4 mile ascent from the old trailhead to the summit, it is the little things that will grab your attention: orange tiger lilies in season, ferns and devil's club in great quantities (stay on the trail!) and lichen-draped hemlocks and firs. Approximately half a mile from the top of the ridge, finally exit the forest and enter glorious wildflower meadows backed by a large talus slope. Look for more tiger lilies, large white and pink Cascade lilies, blue lupine, red paintbrush, and in good years, thousands of white beargrass plumes. Listen for the *meep* of the pika, guardian of these slopes. Though you have already hiked 5 miles of uphill, keep going as the best is yet to come.

73

5.4 miles from the trailhead, reach a junction with the Zigzag Trail. Mount Hood looms massive to your left, seeming almost close enough to touch. Turn left on the Zigzag Trail for 100 yards to a knoll with a face-to-face view of the volcano. The wind blows the scent of a million wildflowers towards you. This is the perfect spot for a picnic. When you can let yourself get up, return the way you came or continue on the Zigzag Ridge Trail to return on a loop via Cast Lake (see **Other Hiking Options**).

Other Hiking Options:

Cast Creek: If you still have some energy left or are backpacking, consider returning via a loop on the Cast Creek Trail, which descends through serene forest around the other side of Horseshoe Ridge. While the Cast Creek Trail adds 2.4 more miles to your hike, it is gentle and quiet. To follow this option, continue on the Zigzag Trail for 2 miles past the Mount Hood viewpoint to a junction with the Cast Creek Trail. Turn left on the Cast Creek Trail and follow it for 5.7 miles back to the trailhead.

26. Yocum Ridge

Distance: 18.2 miles out and back
Elevation Gain: 4,000 feet
Season: late July – early October
Best: August
Pass: NW Forest Pass
Map: Mount Hood Wilderness Area (Geo-Graphics)

Directions: From Portland drive east on US 26 to Zigzag and Rhododendron. Just after a stop light with a sign for East Lolo Pass Road (FR 18), turn left on Lolo Pass Road and follow the Sandy River north. Stay on Lolo Pass Road for 4 paved miles. Immediately after a large sign for Mount Hood National Forest, turn right at a junction with FR 1825 that is labeled "campgrounds trailheads" and after 0.6 mile of paved road turn right, staying on FR 1825 and immediately crossing the Sandy River. Continue on FR 1825 another 1.3 miles, staying left at every junction, until you reach a junction with FR 100. Turn left on this rough but paved road for 0.5 mile to the large Ramona Falls parking lot. Leave nothing of value in your car as the trailhead is plagued with break-ins and car clouting.

Hike: Let me be clear about this: Yocum Ridge is the best, most beautiful, and longest day hike on Mount Hood. Though never difficult, the extreme length of this hike prevents the crowds from discovering its grandeur. They will have to live vicariously through your stories and pictures. You will not find complete solitude here – it is simply too beautiful and too close to Portland for that – but you will not find crowds like you will at nearby Paradise Park. Even if you see a few people or a few dozen, remember – it does not get any better than this.

Begin by hiking the wide trail following the Sandy River. The river lives up to its name as it continually carves channels through the ash of its canyon. As a result, every two or three years the river floods, widening its gorge and forcing the trail to move further away from the river. A previous flood took out the road to an old trailhead near the current bridge over the river as well as the permanent bridge; instead, a seasonal bridge is put into place each summer and removed each fall. Reach this seasonal bridge after 1.4 miles of hiking along the river. Cross the bridge and almost immediately reach a junction. The most direct route to Ramona Falls is straight ahead but for the most scenic route, turn left. Hike 0.6 mile through moss-draped forest to a junction with the Ramona Creek Trail.

Turn right and enter the magical canyon of Ramona Creek. Here the creek drops in chutes and riffles through a mossy, dark forest. To your left are the sculpted ramparts of lower Yocum Ridge. This canyon is beautiful, and you will appreciate it more on the way up. After 1.8 miles on this trail, reach lovely Ramona Falls, a 120-foot veil of water that stairsteps down a mossy slope. You will not be alone – this is one of the most popular places in the Mount Hood Wilderness Area. After taking sufficient time to admire this loveliest of waterfalls, turn left away from the bridge at the base of the falls and hike directly uphill (left) on the Timberline

Trail. Climb out of the canyon approximately 0.6 mile to a junction with the Yocum Ridge Trail at a saddle. Turn right and begin the long climb uphill.

From here the trail to Yocum Ridge climbs slowly and gently through old-growth hemlock woods towards Mount Hood. The mountain is out of sight for the first three miles uphill but its presence is always felt. Hike uphill for 2.5 miles to a small pond to your left. This makes a great rest stop as you have now hiked almost 7 miles. Pass a lovely meadow with a creek in another 0.5 mile and continue climbing up a series of long switchbacks as the forest begins to open up. Look for red paintbrush, blue lupine, white avalanche lilies and many more flower varieties. Climb above the forest at another switchback and round a bend to arrive at a meadow with a stupendous view of Mount Hood directly in front of you. The view is unbelievable. Continue straight on the trail, taking a spur that ends at a viewpoint directly above the Sandy River. Here the Sandy River pours out of Reid Glacier in a series of waterfalls. The mountain seems close enough to touch. This extraordinary spot, 8.4 miles from the trailhead, may be the best lunch spot in the state of Oregon. While this is a worthy destination, I encourage you to continue if you have the energy to do so. The Yocum Ridge Trail switchbacks up through glorious wildflower meadows for another half mile to the top of the ridge, where you will be greeted with a truly stupendous view of the rugged northwest face of Mount Hood. There are no adjectives that can properly convey the magnificence of this place. From here, the trail becomes faint as it splits near snowfields along the ridge before dying out in a rock pile nearly 10 miles from the trailhead. Campsites are plentiful should you choose to backpack up Yocum Ridge (you should – it's easier this way!).

Return down the gentle grade of the Yocum Ridge Trail nearly 5 miles to the junction with the Timberline Trail. Turn left and hike downhill to Ramona Falls. This time, you should take the more direct route back to your car. Continue straight past the falls on the Timberline Trail 0.5 mile to a junction with the Pacific Crest Trail. Continue straight and hike 1.6 mile downhill above the Sandy River to the junction near the river crossing where this loop is completed. Continue straight and cross the river 0.2 mile later. The trail turns right and continues 1.4 mile to the trailhead and your car.

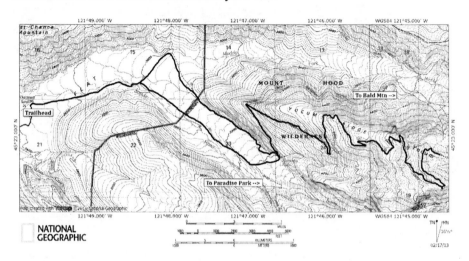

27. Bald Mountain via Lolo Pass

Distance: 7 miles out and back
Elevation Gain: 1,600 feet
Season: June – October
Best: July – August
Pass: NW Forest Pass
Map: Mount Hood Wilderness Map (Geo-Graphics)

Directions: From Portland drive east on US 26 to Zigzag and Rhododendron. Just after a stop light with a sign for East Lolo Pass Road (FR 18), turn left on Lolo Pass Road and follow the Sandy River north. Stay on this winding, paved road for 10.6 miles to Lolo Pass, where the Pacific Crest Trail crosses the road. There is room for a couple of cars on the side of the road here; the trail you want departs from the signboard at the right side of the road, heading south into the forest.

Hike: With so many beautiful trails on the northwest side of Mount Hood, it may be difficult to find a quiet one. Shockingly, the approach along the Pacific Crest Trail to the top of Bald Mountain may be the quietest trail in this area. While you

will see crowds on a worthwhile detour after visiting the summit of Bald Mountain, you probably won't mind. Think of it as the price you must pay for such a beautiful hike in such quiet woods.

Begin by hiking south on the Pacific Crest Trail through a recovering clearcut. Though not the most attractive scene, the open terrain here supports beargrass and rhododendrons in season and offers glances ahead to Mount Hood. Soon enter the forest and begin climbing at a moderate grade amidst large mountain hemlock and more rhododendrons. Snow often lingers on this side of the ridge well into June; if you come early in the season you may need to follow blazes and the frequent PCT trail signs through this section. When the snow finally melts here, delicate white avalanche lilies grow profusely in June and July. At 1.6 miles from the trailhead, crest a ridge and begin descending mildly. Pass an impressive view of Mount Hood and ascend gradually up a ridge, reaching a junction with the Top Spur Trail at exactly 3 miles from the trailhead. Continue straight to a 4-way junction just 100 feet down the trail.

This junction, where the Timberline Trail bisects the Pacific Crest Trail, is extremely confusing. Although the PCT turns right here, keep straight on what is now the Timberline Trail, following a sign labeled "Muddy Fork". From here keep your eyes peeled; just 120 steps (approximately 400 feet) later, look for an unsigned trail darting up into the woods between two large trees. Follow this unmaintained spur trail 0.3 mile to the summit of Bald Mountain, a former lookout site. The summit is now grown-in and all that remains of the lookout are a couple of chunks of concrete. For a view worthy of a lookout tower, continue on this trail another 15 yards through the trees to the edge of the summit and a jaw-dropping view of Mount Hood directly in front of you. There are a number of convenient rocks that are ideal for a rest stop.

When you can pull yourself away from the viewpoint, there is an equally awesome (and far more crowded) viewpoint awaiting in the steep, verdant wildflower meadows below the summit. To find this spot, return to the Timberline Trail and turn left. Just 0.2 mile later you will leave the forest and round a bend where Mount Hood appears directly in front of you. Below you is the valley of the Muddy Fork of the Sandy River. In early summer, numerous waterfalls spill off the flanks of Yocum Ridge (Hike 26) into the canyon below. Mount Hood fills the sky. Wildflowers abound; look for fuzzy cat's ears, blue larkspur, red paintbrush, purple penstemon, yellow wallflowers and so many more. Unlike the summit of Bald Mountain above, you will almost certainly have to share this spot with many other admirers, almost all of whom arrived via the

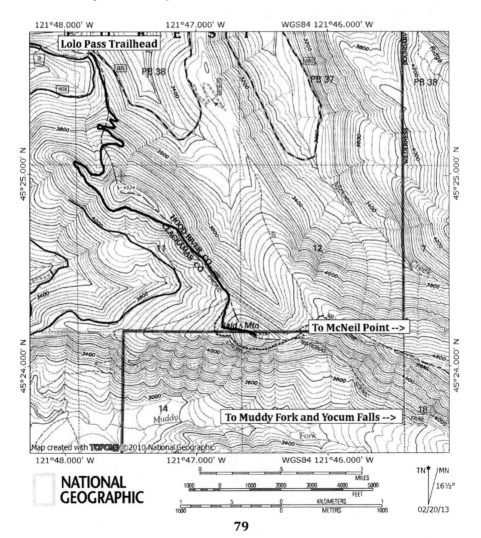

much-shorter Top Spur Trail. It is worth it. On the return be sure to keep straight through the confusing four-way junction and then past the Top Spur junction. Follow the PCT back through the woods to your car at Lolo Pass.

Other Hiking Options:
Muddy Fork: If you keep hiking on the Timberline Trail past the open meadows on Bald Mountain, you will arrive at a crossing of the Muddy Fork. Here the river went bonkers in 2002, blowing out large sections of forest and stacking timber like toothpicks. Above you Mount Hood seems positively Himalayan, larger than life. While all of this is impressive, something even cooler awaits you if you can negotiate a way across the first branch of the Muddy Fork. This is no easy task, as the river swells on hot afternoons with snowmelt from the mountain above. If you can make it across, on the far side of the first fork you will traverse through a low alder forest to the second branch of the Muddy Fork and a spectacular sight: several huge waterfalls plummeting off the side of Yocum Ridge (Hike 26) while Mount Hood towers above you. While you could see all of this from Bald Mountain, the view here is far, far more impressive. Only Timberline Trail thru-hikers use this section of trail (and many choose to avoid it, using the PCT instead) so the chances are great you'll have this spot to your lonesome. Soak it in! When you can, return the way you came.

28. Owl Point

Distance: 4.8 miles out and back
Elevation Gain: 800 feet
Season: July – October
Best: July – October
Pass: NW Forest Pass
Map: Mount Hood Wilderness Map (Geo-Graphics)

Directions: From Portland, drive 40 miles east to Zigzag. Turn left on East Lolo Pass Road and drive 10.5 paved miles to Lolo Pass. At a sign for Lost Lake, turn right on FR 18. You will drive this road for 5.4 gravel miles and another 5 paved miles to a junction with FR 16 under a set of powerlines. Following a sign for the Vista Ridge Trail, turn a very sharp right uphill on FR 16. Drive this narrow paved road 5.4 miles to a possibly unsigned junction with FR 1650. Turn another very sharp right uphill on this gravel road and continue 3.2 miles to the trailhead at road's end. At both intersections on FR 1650 you need to keep turning left (uphill).

You can also drive here from Hood River. To find this trailhead, drive Interstate 84 east to Hood River. At exit 62, leave the freeway and drive into Hood River. Turn right on 13th Street and drive up and out of downtown. Turn a slight right onto 12th Street (which becomes OR 281 but is often signed as Tucker Road) and continue south 10.7 miles from Hood River to a junction with Lost Lake Road.

Fork to the right on Lost Lake Road and stay on this road 8.2 miles to a possibly unsigned junction with Lolo Pass Road (FR 18) just before a switchback in the road. Turn left here, angle downhill to cross the West Fork of the Hood River, and drive 3.1 miles to the junction with FR 16 under the powerlines described above. Veer to the left on FR 16 for 5.4 miles and then turn a sharp right uphill on FR 1650, reaching the trailhead at road's end in 3.2 gravel miles.

Hike: Cairn Basin has long been one of the most popular destinations on the north side of Mount Hood. Despite the nearly 2.5 hour drive from Portland, hikers flock to this scenic part of the mountain in droves. What very few of them know is that there is an equally scenic destination located off the very same trail that sees very little use. Thanks to an effort by a group of Portland volunteers, this beautiful side trail to Owl Point has been re-opened and is better than ever: the views are just as spectacular and the crowds are non-existent.

Begin by hiking 0.3 mile on the Vista Ridge Trail to a junction at the wilderness signboard. Turn a sharp left on the Old Vista Ridge Trail to find the unsigned trail to Owl Point. Begin climbing through alpine forest and then traverse around the east side of Vista Ridge. About 1.3 miles from the trailhead, look for a short spur trail to the right that leads to the first of this hike's four spectacular viewpoints. Walk 20 feet to your right to an opening in the forest at the edge of the ridge. To your south, Mount Hood towers over forest burnt in the 2011 Dollar Lake fire. As great as this is, don't turn around yet! Return to the forest and continue a gentle traverse up and down just below the ridge crest another 0.5 mile to a scenic meadow where the trail seems to disappear. Continue straight through the meadow and continue 0.4 mile to an unsigned junction in a saddle. To find the Rockpile viewpoint, turn right. Hike 100 yards through the saddle until you enter a meadow. Continue another 20 yards through the meadow, looking for a faint spur trail to your right. Turn right and hike this spur another 100 yards through open forest to the Rockpile, a viewpoint with another outstanding view of Mount Hood. If you cannot locate the faint trail to the Rockpile, just turn right after about 120 yards on the first spur trail and bushwhack 100 yards to the Rockpile. After leaving the Rockpile, return to the main trail and turn right (north).

From here, the trail continues a gentle climb another 0.4 mile to another junction, this one for Owl Point. Turn right and hike 0.1 mile on this spur trail to a large jumble of boulders at the ridge end, where you are greeted with the best viewpoint yet. Mount Hood fills the sky to the south. The view is incredible, even postcard-worthy. Even though you've only hiked 2.1 miles, you may be tempted to stop for lunch (or a late afternoon snack – the photography lighting is best here in late afternoon). You would be hard-pressed to find a better viewpoint anywhere in this area.

If you decide to continue, return to the main trail and again turn right to find the last of the trail's 4 viewpoints. You will descend slightly another 0.2 mile to Alki Point, just off the trail to your left. Here Mount Hood is hidden, but you at last have views of three Washington volcanoes that have stayed out of sight so far, Mounts Saint Helens, Rainier and Adams. Mount Defiance and the Hood River valley are closer at hand. From this point the trail begins a quick 1 mile descent to tiny Perry Lake but the best scenery is behind you. Return the way you came.

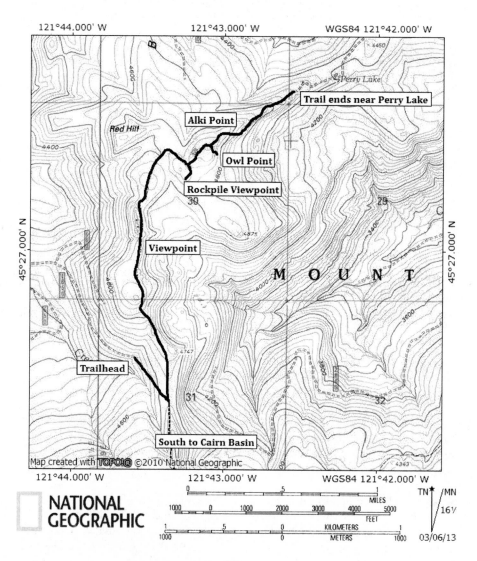

29. Boulder Lake Loop

Distance: 7.4 mile loop + 1.8 miles round trip to Bonney Butte
Elevation Gain: 1,700 feet
Season: July – October
Best: August – October
Pass: NW Forest Pass
Map: Mount Hood (Green Trails #462)

Directions: From Portland, drive east on US 26 for 49 miles to a junction with OR 35. Turn right and drive around Mount Hood 4.7 miles to a poorly-marked intersection with FR 48 just after crossing the White River at the site of a massive 2006 flood. Turn right and drive down FR 48 for exactly 6.9 miles to a poorly-marked turnoff on FR 4890 on your left. Drive this paved road for 3.7 miles to a junction and continue straight, now on FR 4881 for 2.5 paved but brushy miles. Reach a junction with FR 4880 and turn left for 4 narrow, washboarded gravel miles to the well-marked trailhead on your left.

Hike: A deep turquoise lake tucked away in a dramatic old-growth forest; vast meadows of wildflowers and brooks with a peek out to Mount Hood; hidden groves of massive Douglas firs, mountain hemlocks and larches, the most impressive grove of ancient trees remaining in the eastern part of the Mount Hood National Forest...this is what awaits you on this gorgeous loop hike in and around Boulder Lake. Remote and yet easily accessible, Boulder Lake is one of the most notable hidden gems in the Mount Hood area. Add in expansive and scenic Bonney Meadows and a jaw-dropping view from the summit of Bonney Butte and you have a full day of explorations in this little-known hiking paradise.

Depart from the well-marked trailhead and set off uphill on a wide trail amongst large Douglas firs and mountain hemlocks. In just a few minutes time pass shallow Spinning Lake and climb another few minutes to a trail junction at deep, aquamarine Boulder Lake. Rimmed by cliffs and a massive talus slope, the lake is the perfect destination for those hiking with small children or looking for an easy backpack destination. With 10 sites, you have your pick should you choose to make this your destination. There is a trail circling the lake, inviting further exploration. Listen for what sounds like thousands of pikas in the talus slope across the lake. Boulder Lake speaks to the heart; it is difficult to leave.

After inspecting Boulder Lake, return to the signboard at Boulder Lake and turn left on the Little Boulder Lake Trail (463A). This well-maintained path climbs over a ridge to the south of Boulder Lake before gently descending to shallow Little Boulder Lake, a total of 0.7 mile from its northern sibling. While Boulder Lake is slowly gaining in popularity, you will see very few people here. About halfway around the lake, the trail curves to the left away from the lake and promptly marches out to a forest road. Turn right here.

For the next 0.8 mile you will be on this lonely road. While still maintained for automobile travel, it is doubtful you will encounter any here. To your left, views open out to the wide valley of Boulder Creek, headed by Grasshopper Point. Climb gradually out of Little Boulder Lake's hanging valley to the ridgecrest, where the road crosses the Forest Creek Trail (473). Turn right here and follow this quiet but well-maintained trail as it alternates between forest and recovering clearcuts. While hiking through clearcuts might sound unpleasant, the forest here is beginning to grow back while wildflowers have grown in, giving you something to look at as the forest recovers. At 2.7 miles from the trailhead, pass an excellent clifftop viewpoint down to Little Boulder Lake on your right. Hike another 1.2 miles of forest mixed with recovering clearcuts to Echo Point, a flower-spangled meadow with a view looking east and north towards the peaks of the Badger Creek Wilderness. Past Echo Point, the trail descends steeply to a junction at the edge of vast Bonney Meadows. While you can go right to continue your loop, I recommend instead turning left and hiking 0.3 mile to a viewpoint of Mount Hood looming over two small ponds at the edge of Bonney Meadows.

From this point you have two options, one boring and the other interesting: you could continue hiking to the left, reaching FR 4891 just 0.2 mile later. From there you would then hike 0.1 mile to a junction with the spur road into Bonney Meadows Campground. Or you could turn back to the junction with the Forest Creek Trail that you came in on, and continue straight 0.2 mile to a junction with the Boulder Lake Trail (this is the interesting option). From this junction, turn left and hike 0.2 mile to the campground, where you will find picnic tables, nice bathrooms and a few campers brave enough to drive the terrible, horrible, no good road into this campground. If you are feeling tired, you can turn around and hike back to your car via the excellent Bonney Meadows and Boulder Lake Way Trails. If you have more energy, however, I recommend hiking up to the summit of Bonney Butte, an endeavor that will add 1.8 miles of hiking to your day's total.

To find Bonney Butte, leave the campground and hike out the access road to FR 4891. Turn right and walk along the road 0.3 mile to an unmarked road fork on your left. Turn left; pass a gate and hike up this old road 0.6 mile to the summit of Bonney Butte and its stunning view of Mount Hood. Plaques mark the fire lookout that once stood here and give detailed information about hawk migrations; indeed, the summit of Bonney Butte is one of the best places in the Oregon Cascades to spot these majestic raptors. While a ridge blocks the view to the north, the view to the south stretches to Mount Jefferson and beyond.

Following this excursion, return to Bonney Meadows Campground and turn left on the Boulder Lake Way Trail. You will descend through outstanding groves of noble fir for 1.6 miles to Boulder Lake, passing many talus slopes and tiny Kane Springs. When you reach the lake, hike around it to the signboard junction where you began your loop. Turn left and descend 0.3 mile to your car.

Other Hiking Options:
Crane Creek loop: It is also possible to return from Bonney Meadows via a loop on the Crane Creek and Crane Prairie Trails. From Bonney Meadows follow FR 4891 approximately 1 mile north of the campground (or 0.7 north of the Bonney

Butte spur road) to the unsigned Crane Prairie Trail (464). Just after you start descending around a curve, look for a pullout on the right side of the road with the trail heading down diagonally to the northeast. If you reach a junction with FR 4860, you've gone too far. The Crane Prairie Trail descends through grand old woods first gradually and then steeply for 2.6 miles to an unmarked junction

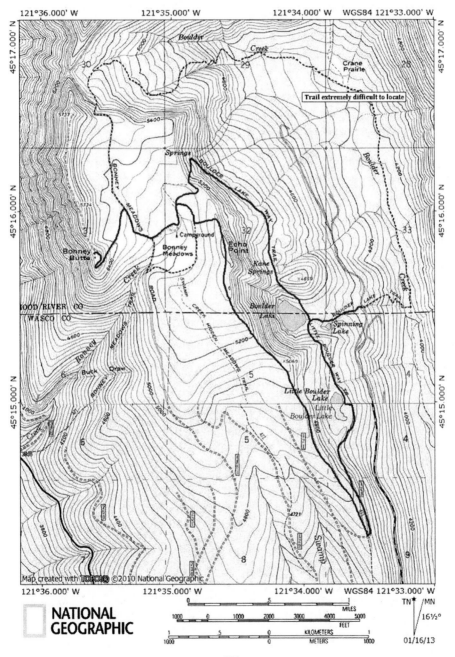

with the Crane Creek Trail (478) in Crane Prairie that is exasperatingly difficult to find. Look for a "5" posted to a tree on the Crane Creek Trail as it cuts away the opposite direction. Once on the Crane Creek Trail, descend paralleling Boulder Creek 1.7 miles to a signed junction with the Boulder Lake Trail. Turn right and hike 0.5 mile back to the trailhead. Please be advised: all trails in Crane Prairie are faint and quite difficult to find; please allow a lot of extra time for route-finding down here coming from either direction. Do not attempt this loop unless you are very capable at finding faint trails and have enough time to turn around or bushwhack if you become lost. For more information consult the Portland Hikers Field Guide at this link: http://bit.ly/WXzEJY

30. Fifteenmile Creek Loop

Distance: 10.3 mile loop
Elevation Gain: 1, 900 feet
Season: June – November
Best: June – July, October
Pass: NW Forest Pass
Map: Flag Point (Green Trails #463)

Directions: From Portland drive US 26 east to a junction with OR 35 on the side of Mt. Hood. Turn onto OR 35 and continue for 13.5 miles to a junction with FR 44 (Dufur Mill Rd.) between mileposts 70 and 71. Turn right and continue on FR 44 for 5.2 miles. At a junction, turn right and continue on FR 44 for 3.1 miles. Turn right on unsigned but paved FR 4420 and continue for 2.2 miles to a junction. Drive straight, now on paved FR 2730 for 2.1 miles to rustic but charming Fifteenmile Campground. The trail departs from a sign on the left side of the campground, near the outhouse.

Hike: Traveling east out of the Cascades, the transition from wet, western forest to dry, high desert is rapid. Hike this outstanding loop on both sides of spectacular Fifteenmile Creek and you can experience an almost full transition and back in just 10 miles of hiking. There is a catch: you have to hike downhill first. While the thought of descending a canyon for five miles and then climbing back out might not be your cup of coffee, consider this: the way back is never steep, and the scenery is better on the second half of the loop. Because you have to climb out of the canyon later in the day, avoid this hike on hot days – it won't be as nice when you're climbing out in 95º heat.

Head out from the delightful Fifteenmile Campground into the pine forests above rushing Fifteenmile Creek, which Congress designated a Wild and Scenic River in 2009. In early summer look for a bouquet of flowers along the charming, stair-stepping creek. After half a mile reach a junction with the Cedar Creek Trail and turn right to begin the loop, crossing the creek and ascending slightly up to the ridge. From here it's all downhill until your reunion with the Fifteenmile Trail.

After 1.5 miles of descent you will reach Onion Flat, a park-like meadow dominated by old-growth ponderosa pines. From here on down you can feel the transition into Central Oregon high desert as the terrain changes with each step. Look over the ridgeline across the canyon for views of Mount Adams and at one spot, the tip of Mount Hood. Also be on the lookout for peach-colored large leaf Collomia, very rare for this part of the Pacific Northwest. Cross a decommissioned road at 3.5 miles and begin a steep descent down into the canyon, finally crossing Fifteenmile Creek and reaching a reunion with the Fifteenmile trail exactly 5 miles from the campground. A beautiful cedar grove here along the glassy, crystal-clear creek immediately before the junction provides an excellent resting spot. If one were so inclined, it is possible to hike in to this spot by driving FR 4421 down into the canyon and hiking the Fifteenmile trail 3.25 miles to this junction – an endeavor that would allow you to hike uphill first but also force you to drive for a very long time on rough roads. After lunch it is well worth it to continue downstream (to the right) on the Fifteenmile Trail another 0.3 mile to Pinegate Meadow, which, in season, features an excellent display of wildflowers and is surrounded by a cluster of tall, arching Ponderosa pines. Return then to the junction with the Cedar Creek Trail and continue straight.

Now on the Fifteenmile Trail, the climb out of the canyon begins with a relatively

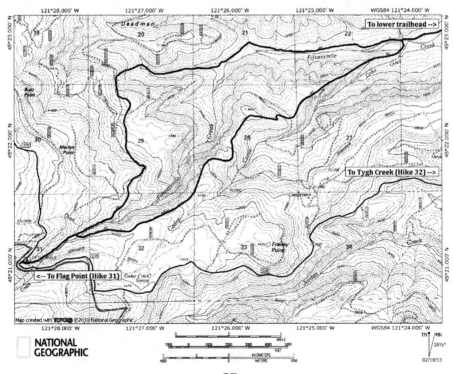

level stretch through flower gardens along Fifteenmile Creek. In summer look for large whitish-pink Cascade lilies, a showy flower that grows profusely down in this canyon. Above you ancient ponderosas reign supreme. Before you begin your ascent in earnest, pass an enormous black Cottonwood tree in a cedar grove along Fifteenmile Creek. Shortly after, begin your ascent. You may have competition for the trail from a few descending mountain bikers but they are few and far between. The climb uphill is mostly gradual with a few switchbacks and a relatively easy grade. 2.5 miles from the junction at the bottom of the canyon, reach an open meadow where you can look across the canyon while large ponderosas beg to be photographed. Keen eyes may spot the Cedar Creek Trail on the ridge across the canyon. From this point on the climbing becomes even more gradual while the many wildflowers make you grab for your camera; look for red skyrocket and paintbrush, yellow balsamroot, stonecrop and many, many more.

Pass by a road to your right (keep on the trail!) and reenter the forest. From here you'll eventually turn left on the remains of an old road and continue uphill, always climbing gradually. At about 3.8 miles from the trail junction (or about 1.5 miles down the Fifteenmile Trail from the campground) reach a scenic rock outcrop known as Pat's Point with a view across Fifteenmile Creek's canyon. Listen for a waterfall in the canyon below. The many and varied rock formations here invite exploration. Once past Pat's Point, the Fifteenmile trail then reenters the forest and climbs another 1.5 gradual miles to the campground and your car.

31. Flag and West Point

Distance: 9 miles out and back
Elevation Gain: 1, 600 feet
Season: June – October
Best: June – July, October
Pass: NW Forest Pass
Map: Flag Point (Green Trails #463)

Directions: From Portland drive US 26 east to a junction with OR 35 on the side of Mt. Hood. Turn onto OR 35 and continue for 13.5 miles to a junction with FR 44 (Dufur Mill Rd.) between mileposts 70 and 71. Turn right and continue on FR 44 for 5.2 miles. At a junction, turn right and continue on FR 44 for 3.1 miles. Turn right on unsigned but paved FR 4420 and continue for 2.2 miles to a junction. Drive straight, now on paved FR 2730 for 2.1 miles to rustic but charming Fifteenmile Campground. Continue another 200 yards to the trailhead at a pullout on the left (but the trail departs to the right, uphill) just before the road crosses Fret Creek.

Hike: The Badger Creek Wilderness is the best kept secret in the region. Located east of Mount Hood and the Cascade Crest, the area features rugged, rocky peaks with great views of both the Cascades and the high desert of Central Oregon. The forests here are fascinating, a mixture of west and east with Douglas firs and Western red Cedar mixing with ponderosa pine, oak and larch. On this hike up to Flag Point's lookout tower and West Point's high, rocky balcony, you can sample the best of the Badger Creek Wilderness in just one day.

The hike begins on the Fret Creek Trail. The trail climbs steeply at first before leveling off above Fret Creek. Look for scattered old-growth larch trees, a rarity elsewhere in Oregon but quite common in the Badger Creek Wilderness and surrounding environs. Though they are conifers and resemble many other coniferous trees, larches are deciduous and lose their needles after turning yellow and orange in the fall. If you hike here in October you will easily be able to spot these beautiful trees. The Fret Creek Trail crosses its namesake twice before climbing steeply up to shallow Oval Lake at 2 miles from the trailhead. Continue another 200 yards to a junction with the Divide Trail at 2.1 miles from the trailhead. Turn left.

The Divide Trail climbs steeply up to the crest of the narrow ridge. As soon as you reach the top, look for user paths to your left and right at aptly named Palisade Point. Both lead out to the edge of rocky precipices. To the left, descend down a rocky slope to a balcony almost directly above Oval Lake. Mount Hood peeks out from behind Lookout Mountain. To the right of the trail, user paths lead to a series of rock outcrops with views down into Badger Creek's long, forested canyon. As great as these two spots are, don't turn around yet! The trail begins a sometimes steep descent down 1 mile through open forest to its end at FR 200. Turn right.

The walk up the road is easy. After 0.3 mile, reach a gate that is often closed. Just 0.7 mile from the trail junction, reach the Flag Point lookout and its complex of buildings. The lookout is one of only a handful on northwest Oregon that is still staffed every summer. Before you reach the lookout, be sure to notify the staffer of your presence. If he or she is feeling friendly you may be invited you up into the tower and given a tour, which is what happened when I visited. The view, as you would expect, is stupendous. Mount Adams and Mount Rainier rise above the Columbia River Gorge to the north while Mount Hood rises above the forest peaks of the Badger Creek Wilderness 10 miles to the west. In the fall, the area's many larches burn yellow and orange, adding fiery color to the scene. To the south, the view stretches all the way to the Three Sisters while the open prairie of the Tygh Valley area spreads out to the southeast. It is truly a view worthy of a lookout.

There is, however, a catch: unless you are able to climb up to the tower, you won't get much of a view. For West Point's equally worthy view, return back to road below the tower. Where the road splits, look for an unsigned but obvious trail headed left towards the forest. You will cut through the forest before reaching the ridge end at 0.2 mile from Flag Point. The view is eye-popping. Mount Hood towers above Badger Creek's long canyon ahead of you while the view stretches out to Mount Jefferson and further south to the Three Sisters and Broken Top. West Point is also botanically fascinating; a form of dwarf sagebrush covers the ground while a small, pink type of paintbrush is common here though rare elsewhere. Large rocks at the point tempt the hiker to sit down for a nice, long rest. Return the way you came.

Other hiking options:

Lookout Mountain: If you've got more energy, you can hike up the Divide Trail to panoramic views at the summit of Lookout Mountain, the highest point in the Badger Creek Wilderness. Return to the junction with the Fret Creek Trail and continue straight instead of turning right to return to your car. The trail climbs steadily through the forest to regain the ridge crest before traversing several rocky meadows to the summit of Lookout Mountain, 2 miles from the Fret Creek Trail junction. The stupendous view stretches from Mount Rainier to the Three Sisters, with Mount Hood in front of you to the west and the high desert behind you to the east. This is a spectacular spot, one you will likely share with many admirers who arrived from one of the three trails that reach the summit.

Flag Point in the winter: The Flag Point lookout can be reserved for use in the winter, providing the opportunity for a wonderful, solitary adventure. You will not see anybody here in the winter – at all. To reserve the lookout, use the website http://www.recreation.gov and search for Flag Point. The lookout is available for reservation starting 6 months before your visit date. Weekend dates fill up very fast for the entire winter, often within days of becoming available. The access route to the lookout is quite different from the hike described above and requires a long snowshoe or ski tour on closed forest roads. For more information, consult the Dufur Ranger Station at (541) 467-2291.

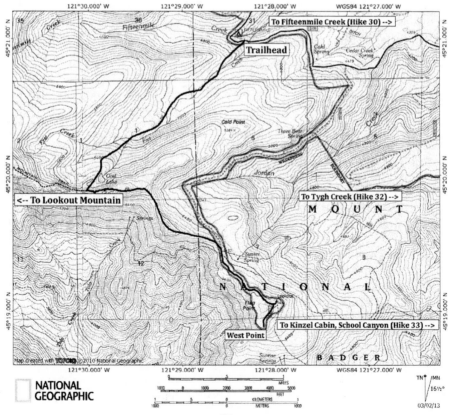

32. Tygh Creek

Distance: 5.6 miles out and back
Elevation Gain: 1,700 feet
Season: April – November
Best: May – June
Pass: None needed.
Map: Flag Point (Green Trails #463)

Directions: Drive Interstate 84 east of Portland 78 miles to The Dalles. Leave the highway at exit 87 and follow signs to US 197, heading south out of The Dalles. Drive US 197 south 27 miles to a junction with Shadybrook Road, just north of Tygh Valley. Turn right on Shadybrook Road and drive 1.1 miles to a junction with Fairgrounds Road, where you turn left. After just 0.7 mile, turn right on the Badger Creek Road and drive this gravel road 6.6 miles to a junction with Ball Point Road, FR 27. Turn right and drive 3.5 paved miles to the unmarked Tygh Creek Trailhead, located at the crossing of Tygh Creek. There is room for 2 – 3 cars in the pulloff to the right. The trail departs from the left side of the road.

Hike: The Badger Creek Wilderness is a paradise for the solitude-seeker. With mile after mile of un-crowded trails and spectacular scenery that straddles the transition zone between lush western Oregon and arid eastern Oregon, there are many fantastic hikes to be discovered here. One of the best is the steep climb up to the ridge above Tygh Creek on the eastern edge of the wilderness. Here you will see an almost sublime melding of west and east and be treated with views from Mount Hood to the Three Sisters. The price for this awesomeness is steep though – or rather, the middle third of the hike is one of the steepest stretches of trail in this book. Bring trekking poles!

Begin by following Tygh Creek for the first half-mile. Given the name of the trail, you would expect to continue following the stream – instead, reach a vague trail junction at 0.5 mile. Here you should bend to the right uphill (going straight will lead you to a dead end at the creek) and begin climbing. The uphill begins gradually but soon intensifies into some of the steepest, dustiest trail in the Badger Creek Wilderness. In the summer this dry, south-facing slope can be quite hot, so be sure to pack lots of water and rest when needed. On the flip side, this slope also hosts an impressive variety of flowers, among them balsamroot, lupine, paintbrush, larkspur  and yellow fawn lilies. Be on the lookout for juniper trees here, at the far western end of their habitat in Oregon, as well as several impressive groves of ponderosa pines. After 1.4 miles and 1,450 feet of ascent, reach the top of the ridge. Behind you, central Oregon stretches out into the horizon. To the south, Mount Jefferson and the Three Sisters loom in the distance over nearby Ball Point. This is an impressive spot!

Rather than stopping, however, crest a small ridge and reach a junction with a user trail on the left. Turn here and 100 feet later reach a large, rocky meadow that is sometimes used as a helispot. Ahead of you looms Mount Hood over the crest of the Badger Creek Wilderness. While this makes for an excellent rest spot, you have only hiked 2 miles; if you wish to continue I encourage you to do so.

After only 0.2 mile, reach a junction with the Jordan Butte Trail to your right. This seldom-used path continues 2 miles to a trailhead on an obscure side road. Instead, continue straight on the Tygh Creek Trail. The way climbs over downed trees and meanders through grove after grove of huge ponderosa pines. The trail here is often quite faint but should not be difficult to follow as there is almost no undergrowth. After another 0.7 miles, look for a spur trail darting off to your left – hike this out 100 feet to a rock garden with a view up to Mount Hood. As this is the last viewpoint for many miles, you should return the way you came. The Tygh Creek Trail continues another 3.5 miles to the Flag Point Road, about 0.5 mile below the lookout (see Hike 31).

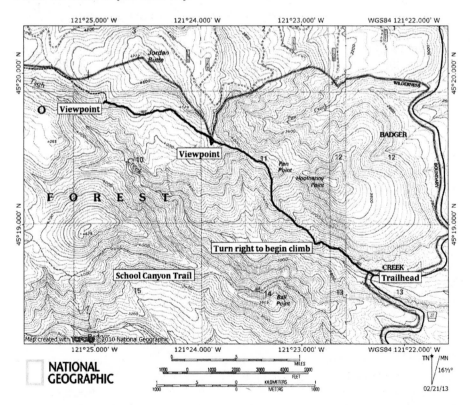

33. Kinzel Cabin

Distance: 7.4 miles out and back
Elevation Gain: 1,000 feet
Season: April - November
Best: May – June
Pass: None needed.
Map: Flag Point (Green Trails #463)

Directions: Drive Interstate 84 east of Portland 78 miles to The Dalles. Leave the highway at exit 87 and follow signs to US 197, heading south out of The Dalles. Drive US 197 south 27 miles to a junction with Shadybrook Road, just north of Tygh Valley. Turn right on Shadybrook Road and drive 1.1 miles to a junction with Fairgrounds Road and turn left. After just 0.7 mile, turn right on the Badger Creek Road and drive this gravel road 6.6 miles to a junction with Ball Point Road, FR 27. Continue straight another 1.5 miles to a crossing of Little Badger Creek. There is a parking lot here complete with perhaps the most decrepit bathroom in the Mount Hood National Forest. The trail departs from the right (west) side of the road.

Hike: The Little Badger Trail traverses the heart of a dark wilderness canyon to the ruins of an old cabin and mining tunnel. Unlike most of the trails in the Badger Creek Wilderness, there are no sweeping views on this trail – instead there are remarkable flower displays from March to June, the fascinating ruins of a 1920s mining camp and a scenic, splashing creek to guide you along this well-graded, peaceful and lonely trail.

Begin by hiking west from the road on the Little Badger Trail. The trail sees maintenance only once every few years so you should expect some blowdown from time to time. Follow the creek closely for the first two miles into the heart of the canyon. On cloudy days, it can be very dark here, something that actually enhances the scenery. The forest here near Little Badger Creek is fascinating and varied, with huge Western red cedars intermingling with white oak trees and orange-barked ponderosa pines. Keep your eyes peeled for trout in the creek – amazingly, this small creek supports a population of native trout that dart to and fro in pools created by downed trees.

Approximately 2 miles from the trailhead, you will switch back away from the creek and begin a gradual climb to a bench some distance above the canyon floor. If you are following along with your topographic map you may become confused – indeed, the trail was re-routed in the late 1990s to bypass a section of trail that crossed Little Badger Creek *eight* times and washed out on a frequent basis. The new trail traverses open forests and meadows that are blanketed with balsamroot in May. Breaks in the trees offer views ahead to the canyon headwall, topped by Gordon Butte to your left. Begin your descent at 3 miles and arrive abruptly back at creek level where you will find a huge camping area. Beside the trail here are the ruins of Kinzel Cabin, now in a state of tremendous disrepair.

Tom Kinzel, a onetime Forest Service employee, supposedly built the cabin in the 1920s. Inside the cabin site you can still find the rusted hulls of some of the cabin's furniture. Be careful though; do not disturb anything you find and be on the lookout for rusted nails and broken glass! Back on the trail, hike 100 yards to a trail junction at a switchback. Continue straight thirty feet to a mine shaft cut straight into the canyon wall. You should absolutely resist the temptation to enter – the roof of the shaft looks quite dangerous. You may also want to resist the temptation to continue uphill on the Little Badger Trail – it climbs 900 feet in just 0.7 mile to a junction with the School Canyon Trail near a helispot. Unless you can arrange a short car shuttle, return the way you came.

Other hiking options:
School Canyon: You may wish to return on the School Canyon Trail, as noted above. Provided you can do a short car shuttle or are reasonably skilled at bushwhacking, this can make for a scenic loop. To find the School Canyon Trail from the end of the hike described above, switchback steeply above the mine shaft for 0.7 miles, gaining 900 feet. From here, first turn left and hike 100 yards to a helispot on your left. Flanked by a fascinating collection of fluted rock pinnacles, this makes for an excellent lunch spot. Return then to the junction with the School Canyon Trail and continue straight.

You will soon hike through park-like groves of ponderosa pine as you follow a ridge towards Ball Point. After approximately a mile, enter forest burned by a 2007 fire and traverse around the side of Ball Point. Keen eyes will spot the Tygh Creek Trail (Hike 32) ascending the slope on the opposite side of the canyon. Once around Ball Point, the view opens up to the rolling tableland of central

Oregon and south to Mount Jefferson. Continue hiking a dusty trail through pine oak grasslands another 2 miles to the trailhead on FR 27. If you wish to bushwhack down to Little Badger Creek, cut off the ridge before you reach the trailhead and hike downhill through pine oak grasslands until you hit the Little Badger Trail. To arrange a car shuttle from the Little Badger Trailhead, drive back 1.5 miles to the junction with FR 27 and turn left. Drive 2 miles of pavement to the well-marked trailhead on your left.

Flag Point: Like seemingly every trail in this part of the Badger Creek Wilderness, the Little Badger Trail eventually leads to Flag Point's lookout tower, described in Hike 31. As the lookout tower is approximately 4 miles past Kinzel Cabin, this is too long of a day hike for most people.

Continuing on to the lookout does, however, make for an interesting overnight backpack. For more information on this area, consult *A Guide to the Trails of Badger Creek* by Ken & Ruth Love. This fantastic guide from 1979 has a wealth of information on the trails in the Badger Creek area and is well worth purchasing provided you can find a copy.

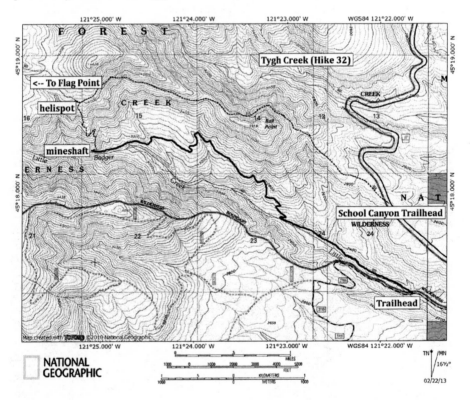

34. White River Falls

Lower Falls distance: 1 mile out and back
Confluence distance: 5 miles out and back
Elevation Gain: 100 feet
Season: all year
Best: May – June
Pass: None needed.
Map: None needed.

Directions: Drive Interstate 84 east of Portland 78 miles to The Dalles. Leave the highway at Exit 87 and follow signs to US 197, heading south out of The Dalles. Drive US 197 south for 28 miles to a junction with OR 216 in Tygh Valley, signed for White River Falls and Sherars Bridge. Turn left here and drive east for 4 miles to the well-marked state park.

Hike: Flowing off of the east side of Mount Hood, the White River tumbles through a deep chasm that few other than river rafters ever see. Near its confluence with the Deschutes River, this chasm climaxes in a jaw-dropping, awe-inspiring waterfall in one of Oregon's least-known state parks. It is well worth the effort it takes to visit White River Falls and its easy and accessible trail. This is truly one of Oregon's most beautiful and least-known places, and it is unlike anything else in this book.

Begin in the parking lot of the state park. From here the falls is audible, and the sound only grows louder with each step towards the brink of the falls. Head straight for the canyon wall on paved trail towards the falls. At the edge of the cliff, stop at a fenced viewpoint above the falls and the lower canyon. While the view here is excellent, it is even better from the bottom. Turn left here, cross a bridge on a strange sort of toll gate and turn downhill to the right. Descend steeply to a long set of stairs near the bottom of the canyon. In May and June yellow balsamroot lines the cliff slopes but your attention will no doubt be drawn to the waterfall to your right. About two-thirds of the way down the canyon slope, step off the trail towards a balcony on your right. Here at last you'll get the full view of the upper White River Falls, thundering 110 feet in two magnificent tiers. Photographers will want to spend at least 15 minutes in this incredible spot.

Below the viewpoint, descend the last set of stairs to the bottom of the canyon. To your right is a condemned building, the remnants of a 1920s attempt to harness the falls for hydroelectric purposes. Take a few minutes to check out the rusting machinery but do not enter! The safest place from which to view the works is from outside.

Below the condemned building the trail becomes rough and faint. The canyon is rough as well, as the White River roars over stairsteps as it rushes to meet the Deschutes River. Sagebrush and wild rose fill the narrow canyon with their

fragrant blooms. Hawks scan the canyon walls in search of prey. Scattered large ponderosa pines stand guard mightily over the rough trail. You might think you have hiked out of Oregon and into Arizona in twenty short minutes! Half a mile from your car, the river thunders over another falls. This lower cataract is less impressive than its sibling upstream but makes up for it with an exceptional display of basalt formations. At a wide, rocky overlook opposite the falls, stop to get your bearings and take in the scene. If you've come for an easy hike, this is your turnaround spot. Below the falls, the faint trail becomes rough and tiring. It is possible to hike all the way down to the confluence with the Deschutes, but you have to earn it. Do not try this on a hot day. Otherwise, return the way you came.

Other hiking options:
If you've driven all this way and are up for an adventure, consider bushwhacking two miles down from the lower falls to the confluence of the White and Deschutes Rivers. The way is rarely difficult in this peaceful canyon. Be aware that poison oak is common downstream, and that this is a much more difficult trek in the rainy season, when high waters can block access to the confluence. Likewise it is a good idea to avoid this hike on a hot day as the canyon swelters in heat far more intense than what the Willamette Valley experiences.

Continue past the lower falls. Climb over a knoll and descend steeply (watch your step) to the bottom of the canyon. From here on out keep an eye out for poison oak, found at ankle-level throughout the canyon. Not far past the knoll, the way (not really a trail anymore) opens up into a park-like grove of ponderosa pine and scrub oak. Cross over another knoll and continue descending, this time less steeply, to an even lovelier flat beside the river. This section of the hike can be muddy in winter. Look around as you make your way for some impressive displays of columnar basalt on the canyon walls. Areas closest to these walls are also rocky, necessitating hopping over fallen chunks of basalt. While this is not difficult, you should watch your step.

Shortly under 2 miles from the lower falls the trail rounds a major bend and arrives at a bench beside the river as it widens considerably. You are now approaching the confluence with the Deschutes River. Rafters often come up this way to camp. If the water is running high you will not be able to reach the confluence without descending steeply up the canyon walls. In normal flow, you can climb over rocks above the river or try walking along the riverbank around another bend in the river to the confluence. Don't be disturbed by the train tracks above you or the road across the river; this is still a peaceful spot in spite of these ever-present traces of the modern world. It is neither possible nor advised to continue downstream on the Deschutes; instead return the way you came.

Sherars Bridge Falls: If you have a bit of extra time before you depart the area consider driving past White River Falls (east) down OR 216 another 3 miles to Sherars Bridge Falls on the Deschutes River. Here members of the Warm Springs tribe fish the Deschutes from platforms just above the river. While the falls is a scant 15 feet high, it is quite impressive – in winter it creates a roar that is utterly deafening. Other channels of the river tumble over ledges downstream some 50 yards. This is a fascinating spot that is worth 15 minutes at least; if you wish to fish however, you are out of luck as this is Warm Springs tribal land. So, thus, the only thing you should be catching here is pictures.

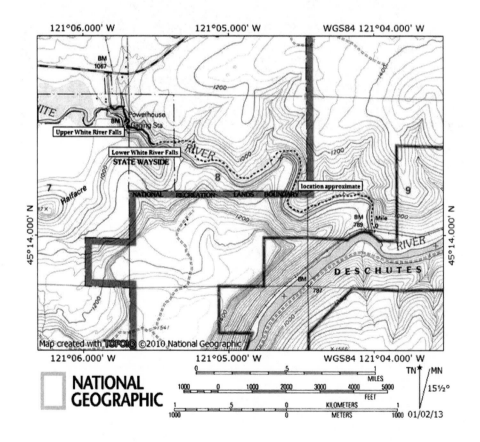

Clackamas River

35. The Other Eagle Creek

Distance: 6.2 miles out and back
Elevation Gain: 800 feet
Season: April – November
Best: May-June, October
Pass: None.
Map: Salmon-Huckleberry Wilderness (USFS)

Directions: Travel on OR 224 towards Estacada. Approximately 1 mile past the junction with OR 211, turn left at a sign for Eagle Fern Park. Go straight through a stoplight and stop sign 0.2 miles later and another 1.8 miles later turn right on SE Eagle Fern Road. Continue on this road (which becomes SE George Rd.) another 9 miles. Just after a bend in the road, turn right at a junction with SE Harvey Road which is marked with a handmade white sign. Though paved at the beginning, SE Harvey Road quickly devolves into a rocky, pothole-filled track that will test any passenger car driver. At 1.3 miles turn left, at 2.0 miles go straight and exactly 2.5 miles from the turnoff from George Road, park in a small pulloff at a junction with an abandoned road angling down to the right. Do **NOT** drive any further as this road is rutted, muddy and is unsuitable for any motorized vehicle. Hike down the abandoned road approximately 1 mile to the actual trailhead.

Hike: Unlike the famed Eagle Creek in the Columbia River Gorge, this Eagle Creek dazzles not with waterfalls but with superb old-growth forest and spectacular

spring and fall color. If it is solitude you are seeking, then there are few better destinations closer to Portland than Eagle Creek of the Clackamas. The massive Douglas firs, the lush carpet of oxalis and the sound of rushing Eagle Creek below make for a relaxing day (or weekend) of hiking in an isolated corner of the Salmon-Huckleberry Wilderness.

The first mile of the trail is actually an old jeep road that is slowly disintegrating. Hike downhill through logged-over woods to the old trailhead at the edge of the Salmon-Huckleberry Wilderness. At 1 mile from your vehicle, bottom out and head into the wilderness. Quickly you will enter gorgeous old-growth forest carpeted with oxalis and moss. Eagle Creek rushes below you, mostly out of sight. You will pass some enormous trees, including one giant that fell directly across the trail that the trail has been cut through.

The hike here is never steep, wandering leisurely through impressive stands of Douglas fir and Western Red Cedar. Cross numerous side creeks, most of which are unbridged but easy to cross with dry feet. After winding through a brushy section reach a junction at 3.2 miles from your car. Here the Eagle Creek Trail climbs slightly up into a beautiful section of forest while a spur heads down to the creek. Choices, choices! For an easy hike, take the spur to the right and head down to a flat next to Eagle Creek. This is a great lunch spot and a lovely campsite, worthy of spending an evening or a weekend. This makes the most convenient turnaround spot – for an easy hike, return the way you came.

Other Hiking Options:
On the other hand, if you are still energetic and ready for more, turn left and stay on the main trail as it ascends above Eagle Creek. You will reach a ford of Eagle Creek at 6.4 miles. From here, the Eagle Creek Trail climbs 2.1 miles, gaining 1,700 feet to an upper trailhead on FR 4614.

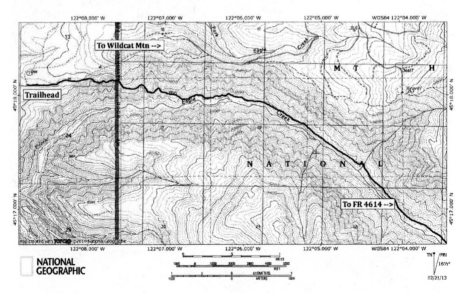

36. Fish Creek

Distance: 6 miles out and back
Elevation Gain: 200 feet
Season: all year except in winter storms
Best: all year
Pass: None.
Map: Fish Creek Mountain (USGS)

Directions: From Portland, drive OR 224 a total of 18 miles to Estacada. Continue on OR 224 another 14.8 miles to a junction with FR 54, the old Fish Creek Road. Turn right, cross over the Clackamas River and continue for 1.7 miles to a fork in the road. Park near the barricade on the right hand fork of the closed road, where there is plenty of space.

Hike: After years of heavy logging and road building in this narrow canyon, a massive rain storm and resulting flood in 1996 ripped out much of the road network along Fish Creek, a tributary of the Clackamas River. Lacking the funds to rebuild the road network, the Forest Service opted instead to decommission the entire system of roads in the beautiful Fish Creek canyon. Today you can hike up what's left of the roads along a gravel and dirt path paralleling this beautiful stream to hidden old-growth, lovely pools and total solitude. Only an hour from Portland and with paved road access, this is a great winter adventure – but then, it's great at any time of year. Avoid this hike when rivers in the area are running high as there are two bridgeless crossings that can be challenging during periods of high water (or it is at least challenging to keep your feet dry).

Finding the trail from your parking spot is not obvious. Walk back to the road fork and then walk uphill (to the left) on the paved road about 50 yards. Look for the trail on your right, which departs from between two concrete barriers. You will parallel the closed road below you for a short while until you reach a small side creek. Cross the creek on debris and reach a fork in the trail. Turn right (left goes nowhere) and begin descending on a rocky trail that parallels the creek until the trail bottoms out in a mossy grove of cedars. Here you will gain the old

roadbed, which washed out just to your right. From here head upstream, passing eroded slopes damaged by years of logging upslope. Though the Fish Creek canyon is regenerating at warp speed, it still shows the signs of logging and off-road vehicle abuse. Witnessing the canyon's recovery should give you another reason to come here frequently (as if you needed another reason)!

At 1.5 miles from your car you will come to a junction. Turn right for a brief detour to a scenic campsite beside Fish Creek. If you are hiking with children this makes a great spot to turn around. Otherwise, continue upstream on the old road. You'll cross numerous small side streams, some of which are difficult to cross with dry feet in the wet season. At 2.4 miles you will come to a trail heading into ancient forest to your left; ignore this for now and save it for the return trip. Continue another half mile upstream on the road to a junction. Turn right at a fork to find the first bridge across Fish Creek. Though the entire road network was decommissioned, the bridges were left in place to keep the banks from eroding. Fish Creek is especially scenic here, cascading through a mossy glade. If you were wondering, the old roadbed past the bridge is extremely difficult to follow as it is covered in a great deal of road debris. Consider turning around at the bridge for an easy 6 mile hike.

Now, about that forested side trail. Hike back about a half mile to the crossing of Second Creek. About 30 feet past the crossing, look for a two track path angling off to your right. Head uphill into a magical grove of old-growth cedar and Douglas fir replete with a thick shag carpet of moss. While the trees are not huge, this place will enchant; stop to marvel at the forty shades of green that overwhelm the senses. Given the destruction reigned upon the Fish Creek canyon, it is remarkable that this grove survived. Consider this as you hike back to your car afterwards. Remember to turn right at the cedars to hike uphill to your car; otherwise you might find yourself trying to cross a huge washout on the roadbed.

Before you drive away, there is an excellent viewpoint of Fish Creek near the unofficial trailhead. From the trailhead parking area, look for a rough trail on your right. Walk ten yards to an overlook of Fish Creek below you as it curves around a bend in the canyon. This should be a mandatory sidetrip!

Other Hiking Options:
The old road network on Fish Creek continues, of course, as far as you wish to follow it. Travel becomes far more difficult past the grove; the creek crossings become hairier and the terrain increasingly rough. With a detailed road map and / or GPS and more patience and energy than most human beings you will eventually reach Skookum Lake's abandoned campground, featured in Hike 39. It is at least 12 miles from the first road bridge on Fish Creek to Skookum Lake, and all of those miles are on decommissioned road that is frequently punishing to hike. This is an adventure best left to the loonies who enjoy this sort of thing.

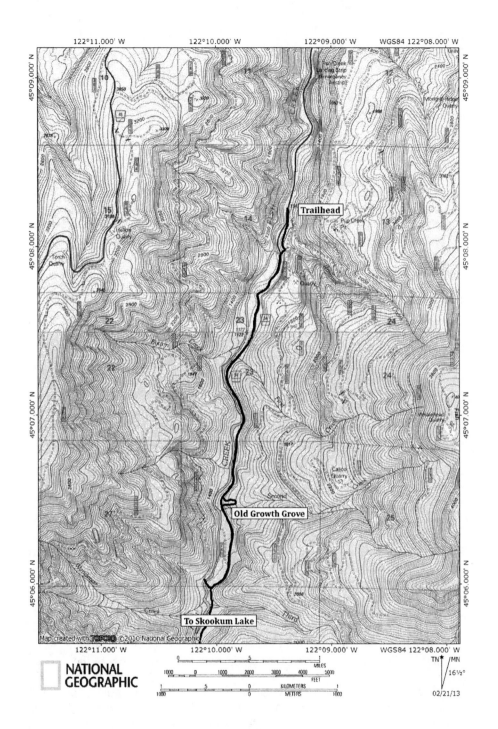

37. Fish Creek Mountain

Distance: 7.2 miles out and back
Elevation Gain: 2,500 feet
Season: June – October
Best: July – August
Pass: None.
Map: Fish Creek Mountain (USGS)

Directions: From Portland, drive OR 224 a total of 18 miles to Estacada. Continue on OR 224 another 21.8 miles to a junction with FR4620 at a sign for Indian Henry Campground. Turn right on this paved road drive 5 paved miles to pavement's end. Continue another 3 gravel miles to the almost unmarked trailhead on your left, at a junction with FR 4622. The trail departs from the right side of this small parking lot.

Hike: Once upon a time, the trail to Fish Creek Mountain and High Lake was among the most popular in the remote Clackamas River canyon. A 1996 flood in the Fish Creek drainage was so severe that, rather than repair the severely damaged and unstable road system, the Forest Service opted instead to decommission the entire road network along Fish Creek (Hike 36). This decision cut off access to the trailhead of Fish Creek Mountain. However, recent trail-building by a group of hardworking volunteers has reopened the trail by linking to an older trailhead, adding 2.4 miles of hiking and 500 feet of elevation gain in the process. The crowds, however, have yet to catch on. As with many other hikes in the Clackamas River country, you'll likely have it all to yourself.

Begin by hiking steeply from the remote trailhead, climbing directly out of the gate. Though unsigned, this reopened trail is in very good shape and is very easy to follow. There are a few spots where beargrass and devil's club crowd the trail (it is advisable to wear gaiters or long pants due to the latter) but generally the way is easy and very obvious. At 0.8 mile from the trailhead top out and follow a single switchback to a junction with a decommissioned road. A large cairn marks the spot for your return trip. Turn right and follow this road for 0.4 mile to a junction with another decommissioned road. Look up the spine of the ridge between the two roads for the continuation of the Fish Creek Mountain trail, heading directly up the ridge.

From here begin climbing again on a well-maintained, wide trail that parallels the ridge leading to the summit. Occasionally you will switch sides of the ridge but the trail is never steep. At 2.6 miles from the trailhead, reach a junction with the spur to High Lake. Consider saving this detour for the way back and continue another 0.5 mile to the summit, a former lookout site. Along the way you'll need to descend a bit from a false summit before switchbacking furiously to the true summit. Watch where you sit! Nails and glass from the old lookout remain. Though Mount Hood is obscured by trees, look out to the southeast at needle-topped Mount Jefferson. To your right (west) is the Fish Creek drainage, scarred

by years of logging. To your left (east) is the Clackamas River Canyon. Look down to cars driving on busy OR 224 and beyond to Three Lynx, the Portland General Electric company town just off the highway. Seemingly all of the Clackamas River's long canyon is at your feet. Though no longer 360°, the view from the summit should still satisfy your appetite for far-reaching vistas. For lunch, you have the best kind of dilemma; do you eat here on the summit, or do you wait for High Lake? It's up to you.

To find the lake, hike back down from the summit and turn left. This spur trail plummets 0.7 mile to High Lake, a dazzling pool backed by a talus slope that seems to extend all the way to the summit of Fish Creek Mountain. There are a number of nice campsites at the lake but none better than the one right off the trail to your left as you reach the lake. If you have the time, this is a great spot to spend a full afternoon before hiking back. Return the way you came.

Other Hiking Options:
Clackamas River Trail: If the weather is threatening or if FR 4620 is closed for some sort of logging operation (as it was one of the times I tried to hike this trail), consider this classic hike. The Clackamas River Trail parallels its namesake, revealing stunning vistas across the river and up the canyon walls. At times OR 224 is visible and audible from the trail but is rarely a nuisance. Likewise, at times you'll need to hike under high-tension electrical lines. Combined, you won't get much of a wilderness experience but this shouldn't detract from your enjoyment. This is the most popular trail in the Clackamas River area (which is why it isn't written up as a featured hike here) but given its

beautiful scenery and proximity to Portland, it is a trail you should hike at least once every few years. From either trailhead it is roughly 3.5 miles to Pup Creek Falls, a mesmerizing 249-foot plunge set in a mossy side canyon. If possible, make this a shuttle hike, leaving one car at the Fish Creek Trailhead (at FR54, the old Fish Creek Road) and another at the Indian Henry Trailhead (which you pass on your way up to Fish Creek Mountain). If you are planning a hike for a drizzly day in January you would be hard-pressed to select a better alternative. Just remember to pack a good raincoat.

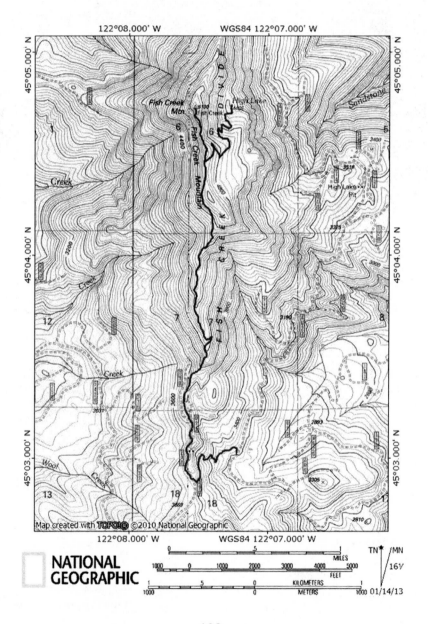

38. Mount Mitchell

Distance: 5 miles out and back
Elevation Gain: 800 feet
Season: July – October
Best: July – October
Pass: None.
Map: Fish Creek Mountain (USGS)

Directions: From Portland, drive OR 224 a total of 18 miles to Estacada. Continue on OR 224 another 25.6 miles to the old Ripplebrook Guard Station. Immediately after passing the station turn left on paved FR 4631. Drive 2.4 miles to a fork and keep right on what is now FR 4630. Trade pavement for gravel and continue 0.7 mile to a fork. Turn right on gravel FR 4635 and drive 8.5 miles on this narrow, winding, pot-holed gravel road to an unmarked fork. Turn right on FR 140 and drive this rocky track 2.3 miles to another fork marked only by a yellow tag on a tree. Turn right and drive 0.2 mile, avoiding a few huge potholes, to the signed trailhead on your left at a campsite. There is room for 3 – 4 vehicles at the trailhead.

Hike: Sometimes all you want is a spectacular view. You aren't alone. Lots of people want this, making it difficult to find a great viewpoint all to your lonesome. This is why you need to hike the Rimrock Trail out to a rock promontory on the south rib of Mount Mitchell, high up in the Roaring River Wilderness. Even better, the hike is a lark – an easy trek through an attractive hemlock and cedar forest. What more could you possibly need?

Begin by hiking slightly downhill to a small, marshy lake. The trail becomes faint as it traverses a rocky, brushy spot around the pond before climbing back into the forest. Just 0.4 mile from the trailhead, turn right and hike 20 yards to a rocky, open viewpoint to the south. Look down to the Clackamas River and follow it for miles to the sharp, glaciated horn of Mount Jefferson. It seems almost criminal that such a great view should come with so little effort. As impressive as this is, don't turn back yet – an even better one awaits you.

The trail continues to climb gradually through a dense, viewless forest of hemlock and Western Red cedar for another 1.5 miles to a marked junction with the viewpoint spur trail. Turn right and climb 0.6 mile to the rocky viewpoint. For the best views, traverse to your right around the brush and out onto a boulder-filled saddle, where the views are unobstructed on both sides. To your right (south), the view stretches out to the peaks of the Bull of the Woods Wilderness, Mount Jefferson and all the way out to the Three Sisters. To your left the view ranges from Mount Rainier to Mount Hood, looming over the peaks of the Salmon-Huckleberry Wilderness to the north. The view is magnificent! Bring a picnic lunch and linger long – views seldom get better than this in the Clackamas country. You may return the way you came, or if you have time and energy, continue on the Rimrock Trail down to charming Cottonwood Meadows.

Other Hiking Options:

Cottonwood Meadows: If you have extra time and energy it is well worth the effort to continue down to peaceful Cottonwood Meadows – just save the trip until fall, as this series of ponds and meadows is as buggy as it gets. Don't say I didn't warn you!

Return to the Rimrock Trail and continue hiking east. Cross a decommissioned road 0.3 mile from the trail junction; look for the resumption of the trail 10 yards to your left. Continue another 0.3 mile to a small crest, where you gain views out ahead of you to part of Mount Hood and down to the meadows below you. Then drop sharply down to the valley below via a series of switchbacks until you bottom out at a crossing of gravel FR 5830 at 3.4 miles from the Rimrock trailhead. Cross the road and begin a gradual descent along less well-defined trail; look for flagging and blazes if you aren't sure of the route. 0.4 mile from the road crossing you will reach the first pond, which will be dry if you come here in September or October. Coming here in late summer or fall is a good idea, as you will avoid the worst of the mosquitoes and be compensated with delicious huckleberries. It is best to walk across the dry bed of this pond to find the resumption of the tread on the far side. Continue descending slightly another 0.3 mile to larger Cottonwood Meadows, where you will find good wildflower displays into September. Follow the trail around the right side of the meadows to the lake. Though shallow and lacking in views, this is a peaceful, quiet spot worthy of a nice, long stop. The lake is ringed by huckleberry bushes, yet another reason to come in September. The trail continues past the lake but isn't really worth following; instead, return the way you came. Combined with the hike out to the Mount Mitchell viewpoint, the trip to Cottonwood Meadows is 9.4 miles round trip with 1,800 feet in elevation gain.

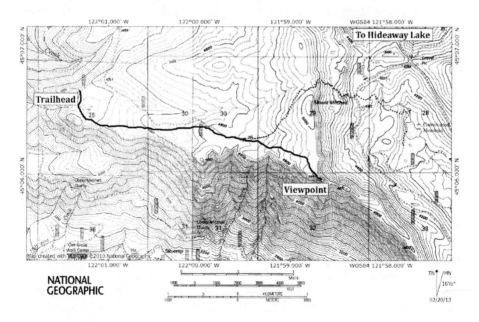

39. Thunder Mountain

Distance: 6.4 miles out and back
Elevation Gain: 2,000 feet
Season: June – October
Best: August – September
Trailhead Pass: None
Map: Battle Ax (Green Trails #524)

Directions: From Portland, drive OR 224 a total of 18 miles to Estacada. Continue southeast 25.6 miles, passing the old Ripplebrook Guard Station. Continue on what is now FR 46 another 3.5 miles to a junction with FR63. Turn right and follow this road for 3.0 miles. Just before FR63 meets FR70, turn right onto paved road FR 6320. If you reach a junction with FR70 to Bagby Hot Springs, you've gone too far. Stay on FR 6320 for 1.2 miles before forking right yet again on gravel FR6322. Stay on FR 6322 for 5.9 miles of mostly good gravel (one short rutted section excepted) and then turn left on FR 4620. Travel on this road for 3 miles to the trailhead, which is on a rather nondescript pullout on the right. Look for a paper tag and pink flagging, with the trail departing straight out of the road.

Hike: This hike to Thunder Mountain and Skookum Lake is the quietest, most remote place accessible by trail in this book. The trail climbs through a magnificent old-growth forest to a superb former lookout site before dropping into a hidden lake in a deep, dark forest. Few hikes in this most-settled part of Oregon offer such a primeval experience.

The Thunder Mountain trail begins by climbing through an old clearcut where the understory is beginning to take over. Fight through the brush for 0.2 mile until the trail repents and enters a sublime forest of large Douglas firs and mountain hemlocks. The next mile of trail is well-maintained and climbs steadily up the side of rugged Thunder Mountain, whose spires loom above you to the right.

Just below the summit, reach a junction with the Skookum Lake Trail. Turn right and climb 500 feet to the summit, once the site of one of the many lookouts in this area. The view remains excellent, stretching from Mount Adams in the north to the Three Sisters in the south. The rumpled green quilt of the Bull of the Woods Wilderness Area stretches to the south, accentuated by Battle Ax's pointy silhouette. This is an excellent place to relax and picnic but you've only hiked 1.5 miles so far, so why not continue?

To find Skookum Lake, return to the trail junction and turn right. The trail traverses around the side of Thunder Mountain, descending through forest touched by a recent forest fire. Begin switchbacking down steeply (remember to save some energy for the hike back up!), a decent that pauses as you reach a sort of rock bergschrund at 2.2 miles from the trailhead. Stop for a minute to inspect this strange and bedeviling spot. Here a hole is being formed in a crack between two large basalt formations. Continue your descent, finally leveling out at a junction with the Baty Butte Trail in a meadow. This junction is usually marked by a yellow paper sign. Turn right.

The Skookum Lake Trail now passes over a trickling creek and then plows through a jungle of rhododendron 0.3 mile to the lake. A landslide has deposited a large amount of downed trees into the lake, adding to the primeval scene. Thunder Mountain's spires cast shadows across the lake. The silence here is almost overwhelming. Follow the trail around the left side of the lake, arriving at a spacious campsite complete with a large picnic table. If this seems strange, remember that this was a drive-up campground before floods destroyed the Fish Creek road network in 1996. Look through the trees below and you'll see the remnants of the campground access road below, now open only to the handful of off-road vehicle enthusiasts who have figured out how to get here. Chances are that you won't encounter anyone or anything up here besides deer. When you decide to return, remember to turn left at the junction in the meadow to hike back up Thunder Mountain, then right to descend back to the car.

Other Hiking Options:
Baty Butte: From Skookum Lake it is possible to continue on forest roads and intermittent trail to fabulous wildflowers and views on Baty Butte. This is wild, wild country despite the large number of decaying forest roads and recent clearcuts. To find Baty Butte, return to the Thunder Mountain trail junction in the meadow and instead of turning left to head back, continue straight. Hike through lichen-draped hemlock woods until you hit the remains of FR 350. Continue on

this road for 1 mile until it begins curving around the forested side of Baty Butte. Here look for a trail headed off to the right and begin a gradual climb of 0.4 mile through beautiful old-growth forest to an unmarked junction on the side of Baty Butte. The more maintained trail turns right and skirts the side of Baty Butte before petering out; the less-maintained trail to the left follows the ups and downs of Lost Creek Ridge. This trail receives little maintenance, is extremely hard to access and is kept open only by hunters and the occasional volunteer from the Clackamas Trail Advocates crew. If you can help in keeping this trail open, please do so! Your efforts are appreciated. For more information, check out http://www.trailadvocate.org

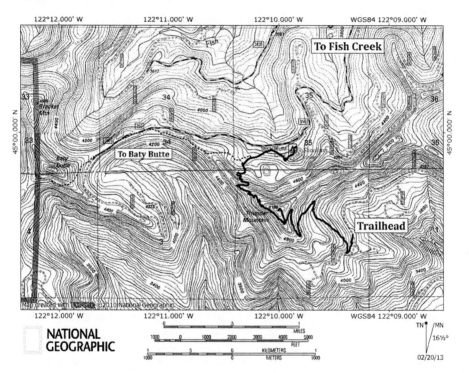

40. Whetstone Mountain

Whetstone summit distance: 4.8 miles out and back
Rocky viewpoint distance: 9.2 miles out and back
Elevation Gain: 1,200 feet
Season: July – October
Best: mid-July, October
Pass: none needed (unless you are coming from Opal Creek)
Map: Bull of the Woods Wilderness (Geo-graphics)

Directions: From Portland, drive OR 224 approximately 18 miles to Estacada.

From Estacada, continue on OR 224 a total of 25.6 miles to Ripplebrook. Continue straight, now on FR 46 another 3.7 miles to a junction with FR 63 at a sign for Bagby Hot Springs. Continue on this road for 3.6 miles and bear right on FR 70 at another sign for Bagby Hot Springs. After 7.6 miles of pavement, the road turns to gravel. Continue another 1.6 miles to a junction with FR 7020. Turn right on FR 7030, which turns back to pavement. Follow this extremely brushy road to a reunion with FR 7020. From this point turn right at a sharp curve and continue a few hundred yards to the trailhead. It is possible to arrive at this point on FR 7020 but that road is gravel and is a much slower drive than paved FR 7030. Adventurous drivers can make a loop of it on the way back.

Hike: Picture yourself on a scenic ridge; below you is the rumpled quilt of the Opal Creek Wilderness, ahead of you is Mount Jefferson and above you are the rocky ramparts of a wilderness ridge. If that sounds like a great time, Whetstone Mountain and its east ridge are well worth the long drive into the middle of nowhere. But wait, there's more! You also get to hike through a glorious high-elevation old-growth forest, a beautiful mountain meadow, and have several outstanding side trips from which to choose.

The trail begins in an old clearcut but quickly descends into a magnificent old-growth forest of six-foot thick Douglas firs. Mosquitoes are a nuisance shortly after snowmelt (in early July most years) but the profusion of pink rhododendrons along the trail is a suitable tradeoff. After 0.8 mile the forest begins to open some, offering views of Mount Hood to the north and passing a few small ponds before climbing to a forested saddle and trail junction with the Gold Creek Trail at 1.3 miles.

At this junction you are presented with two options: you can turn right 1.3 miles to the summit of Whetstone Mountain or left on a scenic ridgecrest hike. For those seeking the summit, turn right and switchback through dense forest and more rhododendrons to a trail junction at 2.1 miles from the trailhead. Fork to the right and switchback uphill another 0.3 mile to the summit, a former lookout site. The view here stretches from the Willamette Valley to the High Cascades. Look for distinctive Battle Ax and Mount Jefferson just behind it dominating the view to the east. Return to the junction the way you came.

For more of a challenge with similarly great views, return to the trail junction with the Whetstone Trail and continue straight (or if you choose not to hike to the summit of Whetstone Mountain, simply turn left at this junction). You will soon gain a forested ridge dominated by thousands of rhododendron bushes. After 0.8 miles you'll reach a junction with the Gold Creek Trail (3369); keep this junction in mind if you plan on hiking the full Whetstone / Opal Loop (see **Other Hiking Options**).

For now, keep straight on the Whetstone Trail (546) and continue on a slight up and down routine on an increasingly open ridge with views out to Battle Ax and Mount Jefferson. At 4.0 miles traverse a talus slope with many wildflowers and great campsites. Views abound. Look ahead (south) at the entire Battle Ax Creek

Valley. Look down at the Little North Santiam River canyon and see if you can find the location of Jawbone Flats, site of the Opal Creek Ancient Forest Center (http://www.opalcreek.org).Look to the left at Silver King Mountain, Battle Ax and snowy Mount Jefferson. From here, you can continue another 0.6 miles to a junction with the Bagby Trail, where you can either turn around or continue hiking. See the other hiking options to continue your day or your weekend.

Other Hiking Options:

Silver King Lake: From the junction with the Bagby Trail you can switchback a steep 0.7 mile down to a trail junction. Turn left on this short spur trail and hike 0.2 mile up to quiet Silver King Lake, a gem set in deep forest. This section of trail is infrequently maintained and some routefinding may be necessary.

Whetstone / Opal Loop: A supreme tour of this area is the 15 mile loop (with 3,300 feet of elevation gain) connecting Whetstone Mountain with Opal Creek's famed valley. While you can tackle this loop from the trailhead described above, starting high and hiking down into a valley (and thus, back up) is not an appealing prospect for most people. Instead, begin at Opal Creek's crowded trailhead.

From Portland, drive Interstate 5 south to Salem. Following signs for Detroit Lake, leave the freeway at Exit 253, signed for Detroit Lake and Bend. Drive east on OR 22 for 23 miles to the second of two flashing lights in the small town of Mehama. Opposite the Swiss Village restaurant, turn left at a sign for the Little North Fork Santiam River. Follow this winding road upstream for 15 miles of pavement. At the National Forest boundary the road changes to gravel and continues 1.3 miles to a junction. Following signs for Opal Creek, keep left (straight) on FR 2209 and continue 4.2 miles to a large parking lot at a locked gate. This is the trailhead.

To begin the loop, hike up the road towards Opal Creek for 0.6 mile to a junction with the Gold Creek Trail. Hike first up an old road then a well-graded trail through dense forest for nearly 5 miles to the junction described above with the trail to the summit of Whetstone. From the summit, descend on the Gold Creek Trail to the junction with the Whetstone Trail described earlier. Continue straight through ancient forest another 0.8 miles to a signed junction with the Gold Creek Trail on your right. As is the case with most trails in this area, the sign reads only the trail's number. Turn right on the Gold Creek Trail (3369). The Gold Creek trail drops to the bottom of Battle Ax Creek's steep canyon via a series of well-graded switchbacks. Reach the bridgeless crossing after 1.6 miles and then continue a short distance to a junction with the Battle Ax Creek Trail. Turn right and follow the creek at a safe distance for 2.5 miles to Jawbone Flats, an old mining town turned educational retreat. Continue straight out of town on what is now a closed road 3.3 miles to the trailhead. You can also skip Jawbone Flats by turning left at a sign for Opal Pool 0.2 mile before Jawbone Flats. Switchback down to the spectacularly beautiful pool, cross a bridge and turn right on the Kopetski Trail. You will follow the Little North Santiam River 1.5 miles to a bridge. Cross the river and turn left on the road, where you will hike 2 miles back to the trailhead.

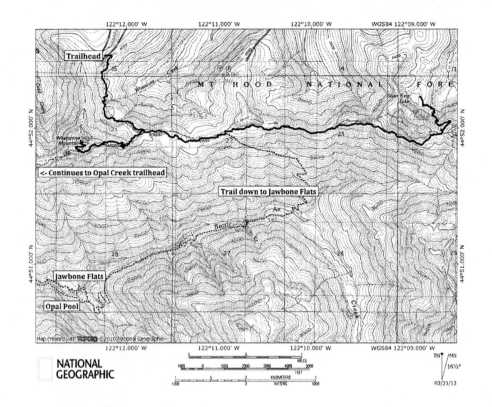

Map created with TOPO! © 2010 National Geographic

NATIONAL
GEOGRAPHIC

41. Bull of the Woods

Distance: 6.4 miles out and back
Elevation Gain: 900 feet
Season: June – October
Best: July – August
Pass: NW Forest Pass
Map: Bull of the Woods Wilderness (Geo-graphics)

Directions: From Portland, drive OR 224 a total of 18 miles to Estacada. From Estacada, continue on OR 224 a total of 25.6 miles to Ripplebrook. Here OR 224 becomes FR 46. Continue on FR 46 another 3.7 miles to a junction with FR 63 at a sign for Bagby Hot Springs. Continue on FR 63 for 5.7 miles to a junction with FR 6340. Turn right and drive 7.8 gravel miles uphill to the junction of FR 6340 with FR 6341. Keep left and continue on FR 6340 another 1.5 narrow gravel miles to the trailhead at road's end.

Hike: Featuring an intact lookout tower and a panoramic view stretching from Mount Rainier to the Three Sisters and almost all points in between, the 5523' summit of Bull of the Woods is one of the more popular destinations in its namesake wilderness area. Many people make it a side trip on a backpack through this rugged, spectacular wilderness, while others hike up on a loop from

Pansy Lake. Very few hikers realize they have the option of skipping the climb from the valleys in favor of a beautiful, seldom-used trail that begins high on a ridge north of the summit. Their loss – this is a much prettier trail than any of the other approaches to this beautiful spot.

The trail begins in a recovering clearcut and as is usually the case, wildflowers thrive here with the increased sunlight. Look for impressive displays of lupine and penstemon here in season. Soon leave the meadows and enter an impressive old forest dominated by mountain hemlock. At 0.6 mile from the trailhead, curve around a meadow with a small tarn; while this is a lovely scene, the meadow is very fragile. Tread with care! Hike deeper and deeper into the forest and climb at a gentle clip as you work your way around the Dickey Peaks, both North and later South.

At 2.1 miles from the trailhead reach a junction with the Dickey Lake Trail (549), which darts downhill to your right; you can use this trail to make an optional loop (see **Other Hiking Options**). Instead, continue straight, hiking along the divide towards the summit of Bull of the Woods. The views start coming fast and furious to your left (east), with a new clearing at the edge of the ridge seemingly every few hundred yards or so. Views open up to Mount Hood and to Mount Jefferson and every point in between. At 3.0 miles from the trailhead leave the forest for good and climb steeply 0.2 mile to the open summit and its lookout tower. The view here is massive, tremendous and every other adjective imaginable. Look out to Mount Jefferson, Three-Fingered Jack and the Three Sisters. Look back to Mount Hood and a trifecta of Washington volcanoes. The entirety of the Bull of the Woods Wilderness is at your feet. Bees and butterflies light on the millions of wildflower blooms that dot the summit. The lookout itself is locked and closed to the public. You may encounter a few other admirers who arrived from Pansy Lake below; what a great time to strike up a conversation! When finished, return the way you came or continue on one of a number of outstanding loops in the Bull of the Woods Wilderness Area.

Other Hiking Options:
Pansy Lake loop: As mentioned earlier, most of those who do hike to Bull of the Woods arrive via Pansy Lake, to the west of the summit. There are two obvious benefits to hiking from this direction: it is easier for backpacking, as Pansy Lake has a number of nice campsites and is only 1.2 miles from its trailhead; second, you can make a loop to the summit of Bull of the Woods, and who doesn't love a good loop? On the downside, this is the most popular trail in the wilderness that doesn't lead to a hot springs, and the ascent up to Bull of the Woods is much tougher in this direction.

To investigate for yourself, it is recommended that you start at the Pansy Lake trailhead instead. Drive from the junction between FR 6340 and FR 6341, keep right on FR 6341 and drive 3.5 miles of intermittent pavement to the well-marked trailhead. From here, hike 1.2 miles to shallow Pansy Lake, keep left around the lake and climb 0.8 mile to a junction with the Mother Lode Trail (558). Turn left and hike uphill through old-growth hemlock woods 1.8 miles to a junction with the Welcome Lakes Trail (554). Turn left again and switchback 0.7 mile to the summit. To make the loop, hike down the Bull of the Woods Trail to the aforementioned junction with the Dickey Lake Trail (549) and descend 1.3 steep miles back to the Pansy Lake Trail. Turn right to return to the trailhead. Total hike distance: 7.8 miles with 2,000 feet of elevation gain.

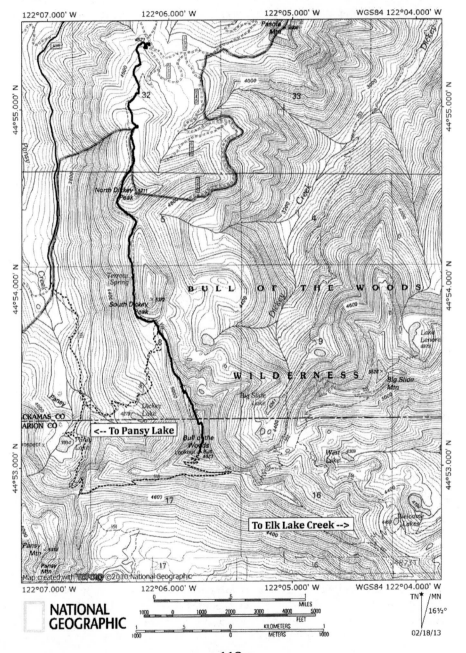

42. Elk Lake Creek

Distance: 9.8 miles out and back
Elevation Gain: 1,300 feet
Season: June – November
Best: July – August
Pass: None
Map: Bull of the Woods Wilderness (Geo-graphics)

Directions: From Portland, drive OR 224 a total of 18 miles to Estacada. From Estacada, continue on OR 224 a total of 25.6 miles to Ripplebrook. Here OR 224 becomes FR 46. Continue on FR 46 another 3.7 miles to a junction with FR 63 at a sign for Bagby Hot Springs. Turn right and drive on FR 63 for 12.5 miles of intermittent and occasionally rough pavement to a junction with FR 6380. Here you fork to the right and down (but straight ahead) for another 2.3 miles to an intersection at a bridge over the East Fork Collawash River. Turn right and cross the bridge, continuing another 0.5 mile on a rough gravel road to the trailhead.

Hike: A secret wilderness sanctuary hidden deep in the Bull of the Woods Wilderness area, Elk Lake Creek will remind you of nearby Opal Creek, but without the crowds. This hike features some of the giant old growth and emerald green pools that made the area famous, features you'll appreciate even more when you're the only one there.

Before we get to the hike, please note that Mother Nature is trying very hard to reclaim this trail for herself. Trail maintenance in this area is infrequent at best. While government stimulus funds helped pay for this trail to be cleared in 2010, forest fires hit the area in 2010 and again in 2011. While the trail seems to have survived the onslaught, be on the lookout for downed trees and washed-out spots when you come this way. In addition, there are other challenges. With no bridges, you'll have to ford four side creeks in addition to twice fording Elk Lake Creek itself. Don't let this discourage you! The scenery here is worth walking through fire and water both.

The trail begins in an old clearcut and quickly enters the fire zone as it traverses a steep slope above the creek. The first views of Elk Lake Creek are attained shortly afterwards with a view down towards a waterfall and the first of many deep green pools below. At 0.6 miles in the trail crosses Pine Cone Creek amidst blowdown from the fires. This is the first of six creek fords and by far the easiest. From here the trail enters the Wilderness area. Once into the protected forests of the Wilderness, the fire damage lessens and the scenery gets better with each step. At 2.0 miles into the hike cross Knob Rock Creek and Welcome Creek in quick succession, a task that is difficult without getting wet no matter the season. Take a minute to inspect the waterfall on Welcome Creek; there are other tiers above the one near the trail! A short 0.2 mile later you'll reach a junction with the Welcome Lakes Trail. Continue straight and soon after you'll reach the first ford of Elk Lake Creek.

If the water is running high don't feel ashamed to turn back. Note the incredible clarity of Elk Lake Creek; while the creek may appear to be only inches deep you'll be surprised to discover that the creek is knee to waist deep, depending on the season. A hiking stick or trekking poles are helpful as the rocks on the creek bottom can be slippery. From here you'll climb into a jungle of huckleberry and rhododendron in deep old-growth forest. At 3.1 miles from the trailhead the trail passes above an impossibly deep emerald pool so clear you'll likely see fish swimming by if you stop. There is a rocky bench above the pool that makes an excellent lunch or snack spot. You might even decide nothing will top this and wish to turn around. If you're continuing, you have another ford of Elk Lake Creek waiting for you less than half a mile up the trail.

After re-crossing the creek, the Elk Lake Trail begins to climb a bit to avoid the wide channel of the creek. Here sporadic trail maintenance necessitates looking for flagging and blazes on occasion. After skirting a talus slope the trail descends down into another jungle at the confluence of Elk Lake Creek and Battle Creek. Ford Battle Creek and just a hundred yards later, at 4.9 miles from the trailhead you'll reach the large open camping area at the site of the old Battle Creek shelter, which collapsed in 1988 under the weight of heavy winter snow. Excellent campsites abound on this scenic of peninsula in deep old growth. Here you'll also find the junction with the Mother Lode Trail near the largest and best of the area's campsites. Return the way you came or arrange a car shuttle to the upper trailhead, if possible.

Other Hiking Options:

Elk Lake: The trail continues 4 more miles and gains 900 feet to its namesake, scenic Elk Lake. You can also drive to the lake (see Hike 44) so don't expect to be alone. From here you can connect to the Battle Ax, Bagby and French Creek Ridge Trails. For more information, contact the Detroit Ranger District.

The Bridge to Nowhere: Close to the bridge over the East Fork Collawash River is another bridge, this one leading to absolutely nowhere. This so-called "Bridge to Nowhere" was constructed immediately prior to the Bull of the Woods wilderness designation in 1984 and was the result of the Forest Service's efforts to punch a road into the Collawash/Elk Lake Creek drainage. Exploring the bridge makes for a fascinating side trip either before or after the hike. To find the bridge, drive to the bridge over the East Fork right before the Elk Lake Creek Trailhead and instead of crossing the bridge, continue straight a quarter mile to the end of the road. If you decide to visit after the hike, turn right just after crossing the Collawash River.

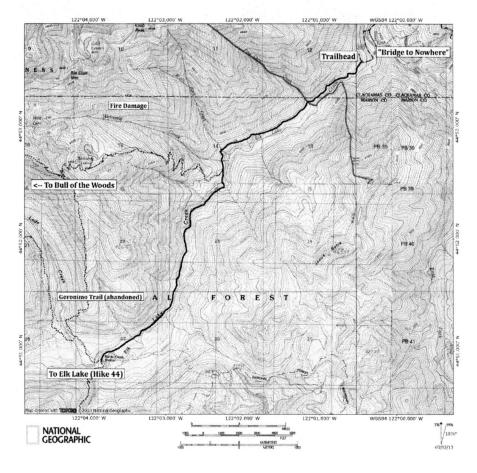

Mount Jefferson

43. Henline Falls

Henline Falls distance: 1.8 miles
Three Pools distance: 0.2 mile
Sullivan Creek Falls distance: 20 feet
Elevation Gain: 200 feet
Season: all year except in winter storms
Best: March – May
Pass: NW Forest Pass
Map: Opal Creek Wilderness Area (USFS)

Directions: From Salem, drive OR 22 east for 23 miles to the second of two flashing lights in the small town of Mehama. Opposite the Swiss Village restaurant, turn left at a sign for the Little North Fork Santiam River. Follow this winding road upstream for 15 miles of pavement. At the National Forest boundary the road changes to gravel, becomes FR 2209 and continues 1.3 miles to a junction with FR 2207. For Henline Falls, continue straight 100 yards to the parking area on the left side of the road.

Hike: Emerald pools, roaring waterfalls, magnificent old-growth and a mossy jungle worthy of Washington's Olympic National Park: this is what awaits you in the spectacular canyon of the Little North Santiam River. While you may have heard about Henline Falls and perhaps even Three Pools, here's the secret: nobody comes here except on summer weekends. The area's low elevation makes this a year-round hike destination and in many respects, the hikes in the Little North Santiam canyon are even better on a rainy winter day.

Begin with the easy hike to Henline Falls. This short trail follows an old roadbed 0.5 mile to a trail junction. Turn left to continue on the Henline Falls Trail (right climbs steeply through the forest on the Ogle Mountain Trail). You will cut through a replanted forest of tall, thin trees another 0.4 mile to the falls, a 126-foot plunge into a narrow canyon. Remnants of a mining tramway can be found directly in front of the falls. If you come here in the winter you will almost certainly be soaked by the spray the waterfall puts off. It is possible to scramble up the rocks to the immediate right of the falls to a mine shaft. The first quarter mile is safe but it is advised to turn around as soon as you lose sight of the entrance. Though less than 2 miles round trip, you could easily spend two hours here – between the photographic opportunities, the mine shaft and mining relics, there is a great deal to see. When you are done, return the way you came or spend an hour exploring the Ogle Mountain Trail (to do so, turn left at the trail junction halfway back to your car). This steep, seldom-maintained trail does not have much of note but is good for a nice bit of exercise.

Once you return to your car, drive back 100 yards to the junction of FR 2209 and 2207. Following signs for Shady Cove and Detroit, turn left (southeast). Drive down 1 mile to the well-marked day use area, where you will turn right into a Wal-Mart-sized parking lot. A Northwest Forest Pass or day-use pass is required to park at Three Pools. From the parking lot, walk the short trail down to a beach where the Little North Santiam River flows through a series of rock pinnacles and deep, emerald-green pools. As you may have guessed by the size of the parking lot, this area is extremely popular on hot summer weekends. In the winter, however, it is virtually deserted and provides the easy access to an incredibly beautiful stretch of the Little North Fork. On cloudy and rainy days the river seems to glow green. You have to see this place for yourself. There is no hiking here, but you can explore upstream and downstream on this side of the river a few hundred yards for additional photographic vantage points.

To continue the day's explorations, return to your car and drive back out to FR 2207. Turn right and drive another mile to Shady Cove Campground. Here FR 2207 crosses the Little North Santiam on a scenic wooden bridge. The campground is one of the quietest and most beautiful in this part of the Cascades, with many sites located just above the riverbank. Best of all, it remains open all winter, providing a nice and quiet getaway even in the gloom of January and February. Drive over the bridge 1.8 miles south along tumbling Cedar Creek to a pullout opposite Sullivan Creek Falls, a 160-foot tiered falls with an emerald pool located immediately next to the road. Despite the easy access, the falls remain an obscure destination – on a winter day, you will likely have them all to yourself. Return the way you came.

Other hiking options:

Little North Santiam River Trail: This extremely beautiful and quieter alternative to the famed Opal Creek Trail, this riverside trail winds through old-growth forest, passing views of waterfalls and Three Pools in 4.5 scenic miles. Though quieter than you would expect, this is still the beaten trail. Expect to encounter a few people here even in the winter. While the upper trailhead departs from the far side of the river from Shady Cove Campground, I recommend beginning at the lower trailhead. If you are driving up the Little North Santiam River Road, turn right on Elkhorn Drive just after you leave the small community of Elkhorn (14.5 miles from OR 22) and drive 2 miles to the signed trailhead on the left. A NW Forest Pass is required.

Cedar Creek: Here's the real secret: in the winter when snow blocks the upper reaches of FR 2207, this road walk is a pleasant and occasionally gorgeous alternative to the Little North Santiam River Trail or a peaceful and scenic addition to your day's adventure. Follow the gravel forest road as it winds through old-growth Douglas firs above roaring Cedar Creek to Sullivan Creek Falls. User paths lead to impressive and seldom-visited waterfalls on Cedar Creek in the vicinity of Sullivan Creek Falls. Following these cascades, the road continues one more mile to a bridge over Cedar Creek. Make this your turnaround spot, as FR 2207 begins a climb up the ridge, leaving the creek for good.

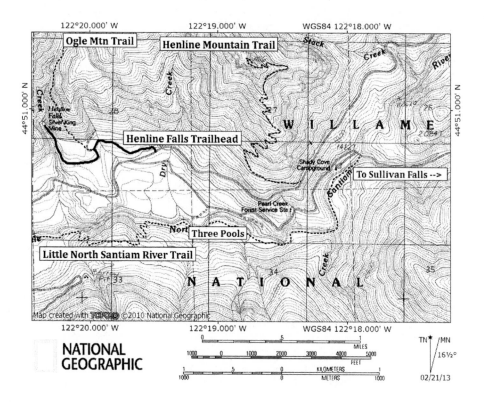

44. Battle Ax

Distance: 5.8 mile loop
Elevation Gain: 1,700 feet
Season: July – October
Best: July – August
Pass: None required.
Map: Opal Creek Wilderness Area (USFS)

Directions: From Salem, drive OR 22 for 50 miles to Detroit. Following signs for Breitenbush and Elk Lake, turn left on FR 46. Drive this paved road 4.5 miles to a possibly unsigned junction with FR 4696. Turn left here and drive this paved road 0.8 mile to a junction with FR 4697. Turn left again, pass a sign stating that this road is not maintained for passenger cars and begin climbing. The first two miles of this road are good gravel but soon the road becomes rough and rocky. After 4.5 miles, turn left at a junction marked only by a green post to continue on FR 4697. Drive 2 miles of rough, rocky gravel to the far end of gorgeous Elk Lake. When you reach the campground, park on the side of the road here; it is possible to continue but the road becomes rocky to the point of impassable soon after. The actual trailhead is almost a mile up this road. Passenger cars may want to save some wear and tear by parking at the east end of Elk Lake, 0.6 mile before the campground. Be very aware of your car's ability to handle FR 4697 – a vehicle with low clearance and good tires can handle these roads if you drive very, very slowly. Vehicles with higher clearance will manage just fine.

Hike: After braving the drive to Elk Lake, one could be forgiven for having high expectations for the trek up Battle Ax. Thankfully, the panoramic view from the summit will cause you to forget the hell it took to get here. Since your car did most of the work, the hike is reasonably short and you should have time to do more exploring around beautiful Elk Lake.

From your parking spot near the campground spur, begin by hiking up the road for 0.3 mile to the Bagby Trailhead on your right. Though you could start the loop here, I recommend continuing up towards the Battle Ax trailhead at Beachie Saddle. Along the way you will trade road for trail until you reach the saddle approximately 1 mile from your car. Here is an unmarked trail junction. You should turn right and uphill towards the summit of Battle Ax; turning left at Beachie Saddle takes you to Mount Beachie and French Creek Ridge while the old road / trail heading downhill follows Battle Ax Creek 6.5 miles to Jawbone Flats. Once you are headed right and uphill towards Battle Ax, views open up at every step. Look down to deep blue Elk Lake and out to Mount Jefferson. Paintbrush and beargrass line the way up. You will pass some strange, fluted rock formations that are fascinating to investigate. After 1.5 miles of gradual climbing, you will reach the 5,558 foot summit of Battle Ax. The view is panoramic, as stated earlier. Look north to Mount Hood and the entirety of the Bull of the Woods Wilderness Area, scarred in 2010 and 2011 fires. East is hulking Mount Jefferson and views stretch to the south all the way to Diamond Peak. The concrete blocks at the summit are the remnants of an old lookout. Take a minute or an hour to take it all in.

Before you continue on your loop, take a minute to hike down the southeast side of Battle Ax to a breathtaking viewpoint almost directly above Elk Lake – you are close enough to hear people conversing in the campground from this vantage point! Then hike back up to the summit and look behind and to the left of the summit block for the continuation of the trail. The next mile begins following the ridgeline of Battle Ax, offering more spectacular views, but eventually begins to steeply switchback down the back side of the mountain. When you reach a junction with the Bagby Trail (544), turn right.

From here the way is easy going as the trail traverses around a couple of talus slopes and passes a few small ponds. After a mile or so, reach a series of springs that flow through a massive rockslide. Here wild rose and other brush crowds the trail while the springs will necessitate rock hopping for much of the hiking season. For this reason, long pants and good boots are a good idea for this hike. Following this section, the trail is once again easy. Reach a viewpoint out to Elk Lake and Mount Jefferson before switchbacking down to the Bagby Trailhead on FR 4697. Turn left to hike 0.3 mile to your car.

Other hiking options:
Elk Lake: Given the effort it took to get up here, why not spend the night at the lake? The Forest Service has spent several years improving both the road access (believe me, it used to be much worse) and the campground. While the road may never be perfect, the campground is now quite nice with several sites right on the lake. Be warned that the road into the campground is still quite rough and rocky.

There is also an excellent campsite at the head of the lake, where Elk Lake Creek flows into the lake. Look for a brushy but decent trail from the Elk Lake Creek Trailhead and follow it for 100 feet to the site and its excellent views across the lake to Battle Ax. Once camped at the lake, I strongly encourage you to explore the area with its hidden meadows, old-growth forest and preponderance of trails.

Elk Lake Creek: If you have more time and/or energy, you can follow this trail through huge old-growth forest as far as you wish. The first three miles are mostly level but fourth mile descends steadily to a three-way trail junction and excellent campsites at the site of the former Battle Creek shelter. This area is described in Hike 42.

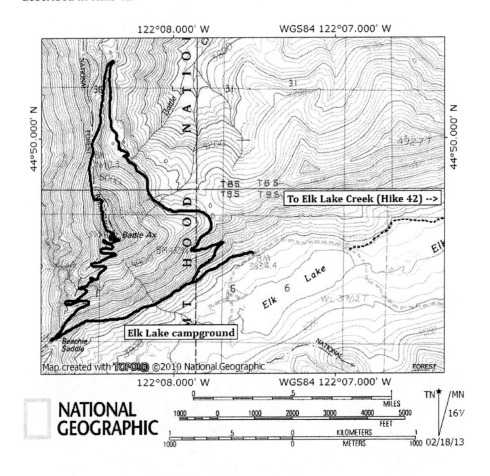

45. Hawk Mountain

Distance: 4.2 miles out and back
Elevation Gain: 700 feet
Season: June – October
Best: July and August
Trailhead Pass: None needed.
Map: Breitenbush (Green Trails #525)
Map note: Locations of both the Rho Ridge and Hawk Mountain Trails are wildly inaccurate on current topographic maps. The attached map shows the correct location of both trails. Also note that there is no trail headed south from Cachebox Meadow, as shown on the topographic map.

Directions: From Salem, drive east on OR 22 for 50 miles to Detroit. Cross the Breitenbush River and turn left on FR 46 for 17 miles, crossing over Breitenbush Pass into the Mount Hood National Forest in the process. Not long after crossing over the pass, look for the unsigned junction with FR 6350, angling off sharply to the left (north). Drive on this well-maintained gravel road for 5 miles to a four-way junction with FR 6355. Turn left on this road for 0.2 mile to another junction with FR 150. The trailhead is on your right at this junction but the best parking is down the side road to the left.

Hike: Hidden on a ridge top near Detroit, Hawk Mountain features an outstanding view of Mount Jefferson to the south. A cabin remains where a lookout once stood, offering a fascinating look at the history of the area and a place to stay should you wish to spend the night. Wildflowers scent the mountaintop while butterflies light at your feet. A visit to Hawk Mountain in midsummer should be near the top of your hiking to-do list.

Begin by hiking through a meadow that is slowly becoming forested. After only 100 yards look for a large clump of beautiful white-pink Cascade lilies in July; these showy flowers have a delightful perfume when fresh. The trail winds through this meadow for almost a half-mile, treating the hiker with more wildflowers and outstanding views of Mount Jefferson. Here the trail is faint as beargrass is beginning to obscure the tread, but the way is never difficult. Switchback away from Mount Jefferson and climb slightly, entering forest 0.8 mile from the trailhead. Here descend into a lovely old-growth forest of mountain hemlock and silver fir and then begin climbing slightly again to make up what you just lost. After nearly a mile of slight climbing, reach a junction with the spur to the summit of Hawk Mountain at the edge of Round Meadow, a long, narrow meadow that serves as the headwaters to Round Lake two miles to the west. Turn right.

On the spur, climb steadily through deep forest for 0.4 mile to the summit of Hawk Mountain with its lookout cabin. Though the lookout itself is long-gone, the recently-restored cabin remains and you may stay in it if you wish to do so. In July the summit meadow is speckled with yellow arnica, red paintbrush, blue lupine and larkspur and waist-high beargrass. The view of Mount Jefferson to the southeast is even better than the flower display. This is a spectacular site! Return the way you came or arrange a car shuttle at the Graham Pass trailhead 5 miles to the north (see **Other Hiking Options**).

Other Hiking Options:
Hawk Mountain via Graham Pass: You may also hike to the summit of Hawk Mountain by way of the Rho Ridge Trail from Graham Pass. This approach is more than twice as long, has very few views and wanders through recovering clearcuts where the tread is frequently obscured by rhododendron and huckleberry. Though the tread is sometimes faint, yellow diamond-shaped signs that read "ULT 564" are posted on trees along the route to mark your way. You will reach the aforementioned junction with the Hawk Mountain spur trail at 4.8 miles from the trailhead, just after passing Round Meadow.

The advantage of this approach is the shorter drive from the Portland metro area. From Portland, drive OR 224 a total of 18 miles to Estacada. Continue on OR 224 another 25.6 miles to Ripplebrook, where OR 224 turns into FR46. Continue on FR 46 for 3.7 miles to a junction with FR 63. Drive this paved and then gravel road up the Collawash River 8.8 miles to a junction with FR 6350. Following a sign for Graham Pass, turn left onto paved FR 6350 for 5.7 miles, during which time the pavement changes to gravel. Fork to the left on a continuation of FR 6350 for another mile to Graham Pass and turn right into a large unsigned parking lot. This is the trailhead. Should you choose to hike here from the north, this hike is 10.4 miles with 1,400 feet of elevation gain.

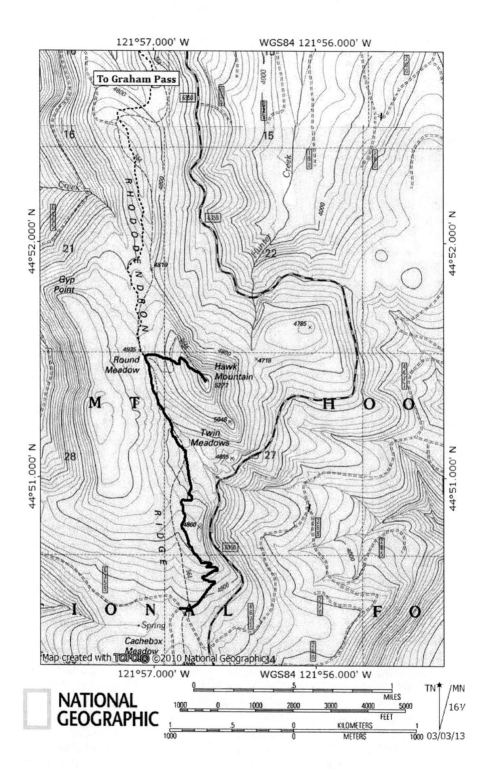

To Graham Pass

16

15

Creek

R H O D O D E N D R O N

Creek

44°52.000' N

21

4819

Tunnel

22

Gyp
Point

4785

4935

Round
Meadow

4800

Hawk
Mountain
5277

4718

M T

5048

H O O

44°51.000' N

28

Twin
Meadows

4695

27

R I D G E

4860

4800

I O N A L

Spring

4800

F O

Cachebox
Meadow

Map created with TOPO! ©2010 National Geographic 34

MILES

FEET

KILOMETERS

METERS

TN / MN

16½

03/03/13

**NATIONAL
GEOGRAPHIC**

46. Breitenbush Cascades and Ruddy Hill

Breitenbush Cascades distance: 0.4 mile out and back
Ruddy Hill distance: 5.6 mile loop
Elevation Gain: 900 feet
Season: July – October
Best: July and August
Trailhead Pass: NW Forest Pass
Map: Mount Jefferson Wilderness Area (Geo-Graphics)

Directions: If you are coming from Portland, drive OR 224 to Estacada and continue another 25 miles to the Ripplebrook Guard Station. Shortly afterwards OR 224 becomes FR 46. Continue on this paved road another 28.2 miles to Breitenbush Pass and a junction with the Skyline Road (FR 4220) to your left. If you are coming from Salem, drive 50 miles east on OR 22 to Detroit. Just after crossing the Breitenbush River, you turn left on FR 46, following signs for Breitenbush and Olallie Lake. Follow this road for 16.9 miles to the pass and junction described above, which will be on your right. Once on the Skyline Road, drive 1 mile of good gravel to a gate. Buckle up here, as the road abruptly worsens into a rocky, narrow, rutted track that requires slow going. This road stretches the limits of what is accessible by passenger car; it can be done but it will test your patience. After 2.5 miles of crawling, park at an unmarked pullout on your right. If you cross the North Fork of the North Fork Breitenbush River you've gone too far. For Ruddy Hill, continue 3.5 increasingly rough miles to the signed Pacific Crest Trailhead on your right. Park in the red cinder parking lot.

Hike: The rugged backcountry north of Mount Jefferson is one of the most spectacular places in Oregon. Though the scenery culminates with the incomparable Jefferson Park (Hike 48), there are other destinations in the area that are nearly as spectacular and almost completely unknown, and two of the best are Breitenbush Cascades and Ruddy Hill. Though short, the unsigned trail to Breitenbush Cascades is mighty indeed. Look up the remote canyon of the South Fork North Fork Breitenbush River to a grand view of Mount Jefferson, and follow the sound of rushing water to a personal audience with one of Oregon's greatest waterfalls. After your audience with the Cascades, you can climb up a lonely part of the PCT to a jaw-dropping view of Mount Jefferson from Ruddy Hill's red cinder porch before returning via an abandoned trail that passes an aquamarine pool with a view of Mount Jefferson. Sound like fun? It should, despite the road access.

After navigating Skyline Road, the Breitenbush Cascades will be a welcome relief. Descend down three quick switchbacks, each passing the brink of a tier of the waterfall. On your way down look through the trees to an outstanding view of Mount Jefferson, just six miles to the south. To gain a better view it is necessary to step off the trail uphill a couple of feet for a (mostly) unobstructed view of the glaciated giant. After you've had your fill of views, the waterfall beckons you down. The first switchback is at the very brink of the falls. At the second turn left

for fifteen feet to a spot face-to-face with the highest tier of the falls, a twenty-foot veil of water. While this spot is nice, the next tier is even better. You will switchback first to the right and back left towards the base of the second tier. When you reach the falls, use your hands and feet to step over a large boulder at the edge of the narrow promontory aside the base of the second tier. Set in a mossy boulder garden, you'll find yourself snapping pictures by the dozen. Be careful, however! The mossy rocks can be slippery and it is prudent to stay away from the lip of this tier of the falls as much as you possibly can. Do **NOT** attempt to continue downstream. The terrain is extremely rocky, rough, steep and treacherous as the Cascades continue tumbling over 1,200 vertical feet. It is best to return the way you came.

When you have finished with Breitenbush Cascades, you will drive 3.5 slow miles on the Skyline Road to the well-marked Pacific Crest Trailhead just west of Breitenbush Lake. Despite the terrible access road, you can always count on seeing at least 7-8 cars in the parking lot. Don't fret – they are all headed south on the PCT towards Jefferson Park (another approach to Hike 48). You are headed north, so look for the continuation of the PCT to your left (north).

The trail ascends through forest burnt in the 2010 Pyramid Butte fire. Reach the top of the ridge 0.5 mile from the trailhead and begin a slow descent into the Olallie plateau. Just 0.1 mile later reach an unnamed lake to your left; walk around this pretty pool for a view of Mount Jefferson and some excellent campsites. Back on the trail, continue alternating minor ups and downs and pass another small, unnamed lake to your left. Eventually you leave the forest to skirt the edge of a massive talus slope (the very same one you passed on the drive in) where the views are massive. Look forward to your destination, blood red Ruddy Hill; look down to the canyon of the North Fork of the Breitenbush River; look back behind you to a smashing view of Mount Jefferson. Take in the view, because you will only get it once (unless you forego the loop)!

Shortly after this view, re-enter the forest and soon after come to three trail junctions in short succession. Ignore the first two to Gibson Lake and Horseshoe Lake respectively (see **Other Hiking Options**) and arrive at the third, to Ruddy Hill, at 2.2 miles from the trailhead. Turn left and climb this absurdly steep spur trail for 0.7 mile to the summit of Ruddy Hill, so named for the blood red pumice that marks its west face. All that remains of the erstwhile lookout is an antique phone box leaning against a tree. The view of Mount Jefferson is breathtaking. Hike around the trees to your right 50 yards to an even better view – Jefferson to your left, elusive Spinning Lake and the North Fork Breitenbush canyon below you and all the way out to the Bull of the Woods to your right. You could easily kill a couple hours exploring the summit; this is a superb place for a picnic! When finished, return to the PCT and hike 0.3 mile south to the junction with the Gibson Lake Trail on your left. Remember – this is the second junction on your left.

Turn left, pass some good views north to Olallie Butte and hike 1.8 brushy miles to Gibson Lake. Before you reach the lake you will enter the Warm Springs Reservation. Here, as anywhere else on the Warm Springs Reservation, remember that fishing, camping and huckleberry picking are not permitted. The azure lake with its glimpse out to Mount Jefferson is captivating. After passing the lake, quickly descend to the Skyline Road. To return to the PCT Trailhead, walk back 0.6 mile around Breitenbush Lake to the trailhead. Stay on the road and obey the tribe's "No Trespassing" signs when posted. The trailhead is just past the far end of the lake.

Other Hiking Options:
Ruddy Hill via Horseshoe Saddle: You can also hike to Ruddy Hill from a seldom-used trail beginning at Horseshoe Lake. To find the trailhead, drive FR 46 north from the Skyline Road junction for 6.3 miles to the well-marked junction with FR 4690, signed for Olallie Lake. Turn right (if you came from Salem) or left (if you came from Portland) and drive this road for 8 paved and then gravel miles to a junction with the Skyline Road. Turn right and drive 5 gravel miles to Olallie Lake. It is 3 more miles of deteriorating, rocky, unmaintained gravel from Olallie Lake to Horseshoe Lake. Park by the campground entrance but don't block any of the sites! The trail departs from site 5 at the campground and climbs first gradually, then steeply 1 mile through meadows and old-growth forest to the junction with the Pacific Crest Trail described above. Turn right and hike 0.2 mile to the junction with the Ruddy Hill spur trail. Turn left here and hike to the summit. Though this approach requires less hiking, the 3 miles of the Skyline Road past Olallie Lake are just as bad as the approach to the PCT described above and are barely passable for passenger cars. If you are in the area though, this

makes for a nice detour.

Breitenbush Lake: Though you may wish to hike around this beautiful lake from the PCT trailhead, the lake is located just across the boundary inside the Warm Springs Reservation and thus access is limited. There is a small campground managed by the tribe that is open to the public, but all trails other than the PCT are closed to non-tribal members. The only way to get a better look at the lake (and its view of Mount Jefferson) is to use a non-motorized boat and float out onto its deep waters. Fishing is permitted with a valid Oregon fishing license.

Skyline Road viewpoint: Do **NOT** attempt to drive to Breitenbush Lake from the north via Olallie Lake. The 3 miles of road between Olallie and Horseshoe Lakes are bad but passable for passenger cars; the last 2 miles between Horseshoe and Breitenbush Lakes are indescribably bad. A high-clearance truck is required to navigate this steep, rocky and narrow stretch, which does not receive any maintenance. Drive at your own peril. Should you find yourself on the Skyline Road just the same, there is an excellent viewpoint about halfway between Horseshoe and Breitenbush Lakes. Look for a pullout on the cliff side of the road. Climb up to the boulders to look down on the entire Olallie plateau, flanked by broad and massive Olallie Butte. It's almost enough to make the drive worth it!

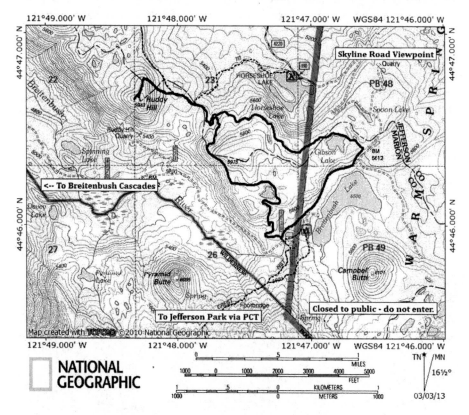

47. Bear Point

Distance: 8.4 miles out and back
Elevation Gain: 3,000 feet
Season: mid-July to October
Best: August
Pass: NW Forest Pass
Map: Green Trails #557 (Mt. Jefferson)

Directions: From Salem drive east 50 miles on OR 22 to Detroit. Just after crossing the Breitenbush River, turn left on FR 46. Continue upriver 11.5 miles, passing Breitenbush Hot Springs. Turn right on FR 4685 and drive 5 miles of level but sometimes washboarded gravel to a large parking area on the right. The trailhead is on the left, at the south end of the parking area.

Hike: While there is no shortage of great views in the rugged backcountry north of Mount Jefferson, few can compare with the panorama from Bear Point's former lookout site. Despite its proximity to the famed Jefferson Park (see Hike 48), Bear Point remains virtually unknown. What's more, the hike is 5 miles shorter than the trek to Jefferson Park, is rarely steep despite climbing 3,000 feet, and melts out on average 2 – 3 weeks before Jefferson Park. So what are you waiting for?

The trail begins in a clearing and tunnels through a forest of alder near the South Breitenbush River, meeting with an old alignment of the trail after a quarter mile. From here the trail turns right and begins a long, slow climb out of the canyon through attractive second-growth forest that blazes yellow and orange in the fall. Though never steep, the climb is continual for the first two miles of the hike. As you ascend out of the wide canyon of the South Breitenbush River, the trail begins to change character, becoming drier and more alpine. You cross several small creeks before passing the ruins of an old seedling shed at 1.5 miles. Continue climbing on rocky tread until you level out somewhat. At 2.2 miles from the trailhead, you will abruptly meet the junction with the Bear Point Trail at a

signpost buried in a large cairn.

To hike up to Bear Point, turn left and hike aside a trickling creek on brushy trail until you leave the forest. You then begin climbing at a moderate grade up the ridge via a long series of switchbacks. The views become grander and grander, with fabulous views of Mount Jefferson at the end of each switchback. The trail is rocky and narrow but the route is obvious. Because the trail is open and rocky, an early start on hot days is imperative.

After 1.8 miles and nearly 1,700 feet of elevation gain from the junction, the trail crests the ridge, turns right and leads to the summit of Bear Point. The view is magnificent. Three miles to the south is snowclad Mount Jefferson, with the Three Sisters and Three Fingered Jack immediately to its right. Below you is deep, blue Bear Lake, flanked by elusive Dy-nah-Mo Peak with Park Ridge behind. Olallie Butte rises over the red cinders of Ruddy Hill (Hike 46) and the rugged, fire-scarred canyon of the North Fork of the Breitenbush River to the northeast. Below you on the right is the canyon of the South Fork of the Breitenbush. Behind you is Mount Hood. With a view like this, you can imagine why there was a fire lookout here. Before you sit down for lunch, look around for bits of glass of metal – the only remainders of the erstwhile lookout. Return the way you came.

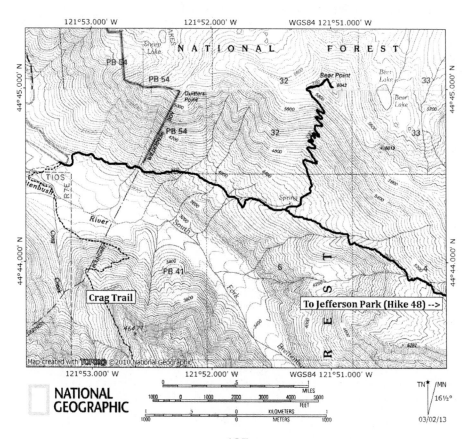

48. Jefferson Park via South Breitenbush

Distance: 13 miles out and back
Elevation Gain: 3,100 feet
Season: late July to October
Best: August
Pass: NW Forest Pass
Map: Green Trails #557 (Mt. Jefferson)

Directions: From Salem drive east 50 miles on OR 22 to Detroit. Just after crossing the Breitenbush River, turn left on FR 46. Continue upriver 11.5 miles, passing Breitenbush Hot Springs. Turn right on FR 4685 and drive 5 miles of level but sometimes washboarded gravel to a large parking area on the right. The trailhead is on the left, at the south end of the parking area.

Hike: Jefferson Park is one of the most beautiful hiking destinations in Oregon. Mt. Jefferson towers above meadows filled with copious wildflowers and lovely, swimmable lakes while Park Ridge's rocky crest dominates the backside of the park. Most people hike into Jefferson Park on a wide, overused trail from Whitewater. While that trail is the shortest way into the park, it is also the most popular and least spectacular. Others choose to hike in on the PCT, a gorgeous adventure that requires a tedious drive on a rocky, narrow forest road and 1,000 feet of climbing on the way out. By far the least popular and perhaps the loveliest approach is the trail following the South Breitenbush River's deep canyon through meadows and open forest. Admittedly, the trail is long and quite rocky but the flowers, views and solitude by far compensate for the longer hike. Mosquitoes are a major nuisance in July and early August but this is also when the wildflower show is at its peak. Consider it a tradeoff.

The trail begins in a clearing and tunnels through a forest of alder near the South Breitenbush River, meeting with an old alignment of the trail after a quarter mile. From here the trail turns right and begins a long, slow climb out of the canyon through attractive second-growth forest that blazes yellow and orange in the fall. Though never steep, the climb is continual for the first two miles of the hike. As you ascend out of the wide canyon of the South Breitenbush River, the trail begins to change character, becoming drier and more alpine. You cross several small creeks before passing the ruins of an old seedling shed at 1.5 miles. Continue climbing on rocky tread until you level out somewhat. At 2.2 miles from the trailhead, you will abruptly meet the junction with the Bear Point Trail (Hike 47) at a signpost buried in a large cairn. Continue straight on the main trail towards Jefferson Park.

The trail ascends gently through opening forest with glimpses out to the canyon below, the ridge above and Mt. Jefferson right in front of you. As the forest grows up it is slowly erasing the great views of the mountain that used to dominate this section of the trail. Views can be had with a bit of off-trail travel but, of course, you'll have plenty later as well. At 4 miles from the trailhead pass a gorgeous, seemingly endless meadow of wildflowers beside a trickle of a creek to the left. Look for the flowers that will dominate the rest of the hike: red paintbrush, blue lupine, purple aster and a flourish of pink monkeyflower along the creek.

The next two miles are a feast of the senses. Mt. Jefferson is in full view most of the way, looming large over the surrounding forest, ridge and canyon. Pass a shallow tarn at 4.5 miles in and hike up to a crest at 5 miles. Near the crest the trail curves gently to the right; if you are hiking in the snow beware of this curve. If you are tiring and wish to stop rather than continuing on to Jefferson Park, leave the trail at the curve and scramble to the top of the knoll above for a spectacular view of Mt. Jefferson. Otherwise, continue on towards the Park along the trail. The South Breitenbush Trail drops quickly into the meadows on the north end of Jefferson Park where it's flat going until you meet the Pacific Crest Trail at 6.5 miles.

If you have any energy left, explorations are a must. At a campsite at approximately 5.8 miles, turn right and follow user paths through fields of wildflowers to Park, Rock, Scout and Bays Lakes. You'll see far more people over on that end of the area, where the PCT enters from the south. When you reach the PCT, turn left to follow it to its junction with the South Breitenbush Trail, where you then turn left again to return to the trailhead. Other user paths lead to Russell Lake, hidden meadows and secluded flower gardens. Despite its popularity, you can escape the hordes provided you avoid Scout and Bays Lakes. Spending a night or two here is highly recommended – the campsites are many, the sunsets absolutely epic and the scenery almost unbeatable. Coming here for just a day is in many ways the ultimate tease.

Return the way you came.

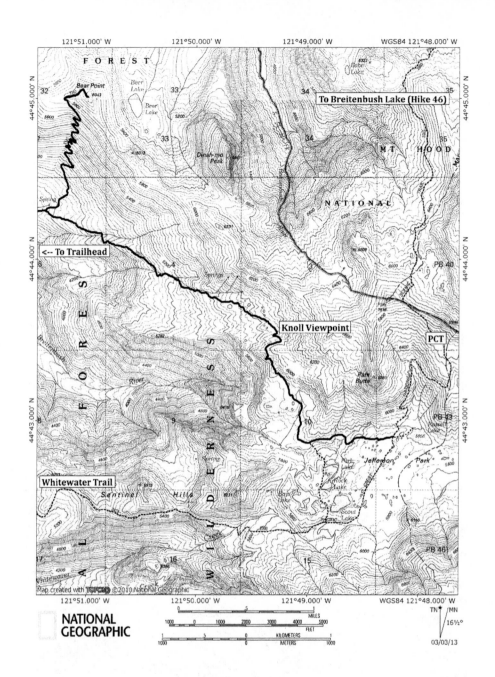

To Breitenbush Lake (Hike 46)

<-- To Trailhead

Knoll Viewpoint

PCT

Whitewater Trail

NATIONAL GEOGRAPHIC

121°51.000' W 121°50.000' W 121°49.000' W WGS84 121°48.000' W

MILES
FEET
KILOMETERS
METERS

TN / MN
16½°
03/03/13

49. Wild Cheat Meadow / Triangulation Peak

Distance: 12.2 miles out and back
Elevation Gain: 2,500 feet
Season: June – October
Best: July and August
Trailhead Pass: None needed.
Map: Mount Jefferson Wilderness (Geo-Graphics)

Directions: From Salem, drive east on OR 22 for 59 miles (or 10.5 miles past Detroit) to a junction with Whitewater Road (FR 2243). Turn left here and drive this potholed but well-maintained gravel road 3.3 miles to a bridge over Cheat Creek. The trailhead is on the left, where the road crosses Cheat Creek. There is room for 2-3 cars here.

Hike: Close your eyes and imagine the perfect hike. Chances are this hike will involve some combination of a rushing stream, huge old-growth forest, hillsides covered with wildflowers of all colors and varieties, spectacular, far-reaching mountain views and complete and utter solitude. On this long but utterly spectacular hike up Cheat Creek to the summit of Triangulation Peak, you can experience something close to perfection. It simply does not get much better than this. While a well-known trail reaches the summit of Triangulation Peak from the west, this trek proves that easier is not always better.

Begin by first following, then leaving tumbling Cheat Creek as you climb deep into a forest of tall and massive Douglas fir and hemlock. Occasionally you will approach Cheat Creek but for the most part it stays out of sight to your right as you ascend steeply through the woods. The grade alternates between level and very steep and is seldom anywhere in between. Eventually the way begins to level out and the forest is more impressive with each step. At approximately 2.4 miles from the trailhead, reach Wild Cheat Meadow, a long, wide prairie. The trail is vague through the meadow but straight as an arrow. As you approach the meadow it appears to be devoid of flowers but as soon as you enter, they appear: look for paintbrush, lupine, corn lilies, cat's ears, buttercups, yellow monkeyflower and perhaps the largest patch of red columbine I have ever seen. If you are out for a shorter hike, you would be hard pressed to find a better (and quieter) destination than this. If you come early in the morning or evening you may even surprise a herd of elk that has been sighted here.

Upon leaving the meadow, look for the continuation of the Cheat Creek Trail, marked only by a red "X" posted to a tree. The trail is tricky to follow for the first 0.2 mile after exiting the meadow as it crosses a creekbed amidst blowdown. Keep an eye out here as the trail bends to the north, away from the flats east of the meadow. If you are paying attention you should not lose the trail. Soon you will begin climbing on a rocky, frequently-wet stretch of trail before topping out onto the ridge. Some 2.9 miles from the trailhead, reach a signed junction with the Triangulation Trail. Turn left.

Just 100 yards past the trail junction, look for an opening to your right. Take a minute here to follow user paths 50 feet to a nice campsite overlooking the Breitenbush backcountry to your north – this makes for a nicer rest stop than anything since Wild Cheat Meadow. Once you have returned to the Triangulation Trail and resumed your hike west, pass through lichen-draped hemlock woods where the trail can be quite brushy (the trail is uniformly brushy through the forested parts of this trail). Small meadows offer your first taste of what's to come: views out to the Cascades and spectacular wildflower displays in July and August. Once you pass a junction with the abandoned Devil's Peak Trail 0.9 mile from the Cheat Creek junction, these small meadows become the rule rather than the exception. You could spend hours trying to count the varieties found on these slopes as you head west: scarlet gilia, red paintbrush, yellow arnica, fuzzy white cat's ears, pink and violet penstemon and so many others. Most impressive of all, blue and purple larkspur covers the hillside for the entirety of this ridge in displays that are almost unparalleled. If you've ever hiked Dog Mountain in the Gorge for its balsamroot display, this is its larkspur equivalent. Looming above the flowers ahead of you is your destination, cliffy Triangulation Peak, with Boca Cave located just below the summit. Don't get ahead of yourself – you still have 1.5 miles to go!

Once you've seen the summit ahead of you, the next mile will seem like an eternity. The trail re-enters forest as it traverses around the cliffy north side of Triangulation Peak. You will pass the base of a rock spire and then traverse a talus slope before you reach the base of a second rock spire, this one named Spire Rock. Just 0.1 mile past the base of Spire Rock, reach an unsigned junction with the Triangulation Peak Trail to your left. This junction is difficult to see as the Triangulation Peak Trail heads uphill at a sharp angle to your left, almost behind you; you will know you've gone too far if the trail you are hiking is suddenly well-maintained and about twice as wide. If you miss the turnoff, turn around and hike back towards Spire Rock. Once you've located the spur trail to the summit, hike 0.6 of very well-maintained trail to the summit of Triangulation Peak. You may even see some people here, as the western Triangulation trailhead is just 2 miles away. The views from the summit are astounding. Snowpeaks from Mount Hood to Diamond Peak are visible on clear days while hulking Mount Jefferson dominates the eastern horizon just seven miles away. The view is truly panoramic and invites a long break just to take it all in.

Before you begin the long hike back to your car, I encourage you to investigate Boca Cave, with its framed view of Mount Jefferson. To find the cave, retrace your steps back from the summit 200 yards to a saddle. Look for user paths branching off to your right here. Make your way down the steep slope here and bend back to your left, traversing the cliff edge 100 yards to the cave. If it is possible to find a more spectacular lunch spot than the summit, this is it. Please do not disturb anything inside of the cave – not only is it federally protected, but it is quite fragile. Do not try to scramble down the hillside from the cave back to the Triangulation Trail – a fall here would be dire.

Return the way you came or arrange a car shuttle down to the more popular

Triangulation Peak Trail to the west. Given how beautiful the way here was, I recommend retracing your steps back to Cheat Creek. The return trip offers everything you saw on the way up, but this time Mount Jefferson is ahead of you – a welcome companion indeed. If this isn't the perfect hike, it's darn near close. More than anything, it proves that easier isn't always better.

Other Hiking Options:

Triangulation Peak from the lower trailhead: As mentioned above, there is an easier way to the summit of Triangulation Peak. To find this lower trailhead, drive 6.2 miles past Detroit to a junction with McCoy Creek Road (FR 2233). Turn left and drive this road for 4.2 paved and 3.8 gravel miles to a junction with gravel side road 635. This is the trailhead. Walk down this road about 20 yards to the trail, which will be on your right. Follow the Triangulation Peak Trail through the forest 1.5 miles to the junction described above. Veer to the right 0.6 mile to reach the summit.

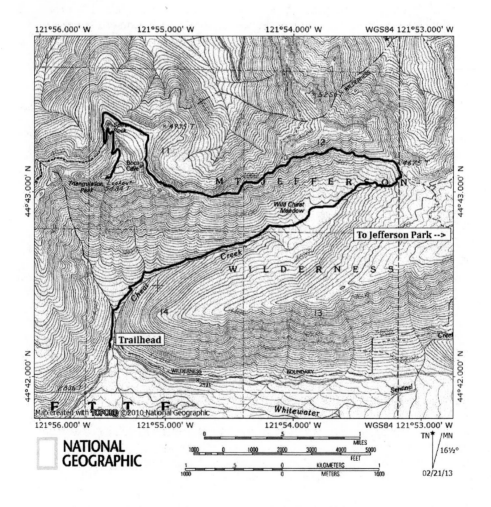

50. Table Lake

Distance: 18.6 miles out and back
Elevation Gain: 2,600 feet
Season: August – early October
Best: late August
Trailhead Pass: None needed.
Map: Mount Jefferson Wilderness (Geo-Graphics)

Directions: From Salem, drive east on OR 22 for 64 miles (or 15 miles past Detroit) to a junction with Minto Road (FR 2253). Turn left and drive this windy gravel road 5.5 miles to road's end at the Bingham Ridge Trail.

Hike: Every hiker has a personal Shangri-La, a place that occupies dreams and keeps the fires stoked through our long, rainy winters. Anybody who has ever seen Table Lake at peak flower season can testify that this lonely corner of the Mount Jefferson Wilderness is about as close to Shangri-La as one can find in Oregon. Just like that mythical valley, this Shangri-La is exceedingly difficult to reach – at over 9 miles from the nearest road, it is perhaps the most remote place in northwest Oregon. Because of the length of the approach, which also includes 1.4 miles of faint and at times extremely rough trail, plan on three full days to visit this magical place.

Begin on the Bingham Ridge Trail. Ascend steeply through a mountain hemlock forest lined with rhododendron and beargrass until the trail levels and you break out into forest burned in the 2006 Puzzle fire. Views of Three-Fingered Jack tantalizes through the burned trees. At 3.4 miles from the trailhead, reach a junction with the Lake of the Woods Trail. Turn left here and begin traversing around a ridge. You will soon leave the burn behind and before long, you will round a bend with your first great view: Mount Jefferson, looming over trail-less and forested Bingham Basin. Past this viewpoint you begin a slight descent into the upper reaches of the basin. Pass a pond with a nice reflection of Mount Jefferson and in just a few tenths of a mile, reach a campsite beside shallow Papoose Lake, backed by a tremendous rockslide. This is near the halfway point of this trek and makes for an excellent lunch stop. After leaving the lake, you ascend at a moderate pace to a junction with the Hunts Creek Trail at 5.6 miles. Turn a sharp right here and begin the steep climb to a gap in the ridge crest, which you gain at 6.1 miles from the trailhead.

Up to this point you might be questioning why I chose to include this long trek in *Off the Beaten Trail*. Well, when you round the bend after reaching the crest of the ridge, you will see why immediately: here is the first great view of the hike and one of the truly fantastic views of the Mount Jefferson Wilderness: the pointed spires of Mount Jefferson, towering over the meadows and lakes of Hunts Cove. Though this section of the Hunts Creek Trail is popular with backpackers, they have all arrived via the Hunts Cove basin, which requires a special access permit to enter (you, however, do not need a permit to hike this section of trail). Hike along the ridge, soaking in the stupendous views and copious wildflowers, until you descend gently to a meadow-filled plateau. At 7.2 miles from the trailhead, you reach a junction with the Pacific Crest Trail. Turn right here.

Begin a gentle ascent up through hemlock forest and open meadows strewn with volcanic rock. Here is where you should begin looking closely for the unsigned connector trail that will take you to Table Lake. This trail is not easy to find. At exactly 0.47 mile from the last trail junction, the switchbacks end as you enter a long meadow. Ahead of you, the trail continues in a straight line. Approximately 40 feet from the meadow entrance, look for a small cairn on the left side of the trail. If the cairn is not there, you should look for a small clump of trees on the left side of the PCT about 20 feet past where the cairn should be. When you reach this point, make an abrupt left turn and look for a very faint path cutting straight through the meadow in front of you towards the edge of the ridge. Mount Jefferson should be visible through the trees to your left (north). If you cannot locate this trail from the PCT and you begin switchbacking again through forest, you have gone too far. Turn around and look for the junction going the opposite direction.

Once you have found the trail, hike almost due northeast through the meadow until the trail becomes more apparent. You will hike through a narrow band of trees to a second meadow where lupine grows in great profusion to the edge of the ridge. Cut through a short band of forest until you can see your destination ahead of you: the basin between Cathedral Rocks, the Table and an unnamed cinder cone. The tread is very distinct here as you begin a steep descent through a hanging meadow that is overflowing with wildflowers. The trail loses nearly 300 feet of elevation in short order as it plummets into the magnificent volcanic terrain of this hidden valley. The trail is extremely steep near the bottom of your

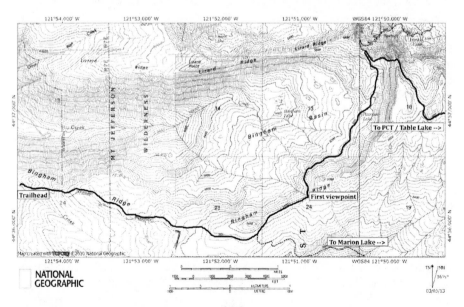

descent, so trekking poles or a walking stick is a good idea.

Once at the valley floor, the trail becomes faint once again – if you cannot find the trail, you should angle to your left around the cinder cone (do not turn right at the valley bottom into a large boulder field!). Cairns help guide you through the valley. Pass two small ponds and a few snowfields as you head towards an obvious gap between the Table (the plateau above the rockslides to your left) and the unnamed cinder cone to your right. If you manage to lose the trail, aim for the gap between the Table and the cinder cone and you will soon re-locate the tread. Begin a climb through the gap and then descend the far side of the cinder cone where the connector trail at last becomes quite obvious. Past this point, the connector trail is for the most part distinct as you alternate meadows with short stretches of forest. You then angle to the northeast again to a final meadow, where you abruptly meet the Cabot Lake Trail exactly 1.42 miles from the Pacific Crest Trail. Make a note of this location or take a photo for the return trip. Turn left on this trail and less than 0.2 mile later, reach Shangri-La: the magnificent aquamarine waters of Table Lake.

Though seemingly isolated, Table Lake has long been a favored destination in the Mount Jefferson area. The faint connector trail you just hiked was in fact a historic trail used by Indians to traverse from Hunts Cove to Table Lake and likely down to the dry forests of the Metolius River. Without a doubt, the area owes its solitude to its remoteness. There are many great campsites around the lake and you will likely be able to choose to your heart's desire even on August weekends. The best views of Mount Jefferson from the lake are located on the southeast side, though the mountain peers out from behind the ridge at many spots around the lake. Once you have set up camp, explorations are an absolute must.

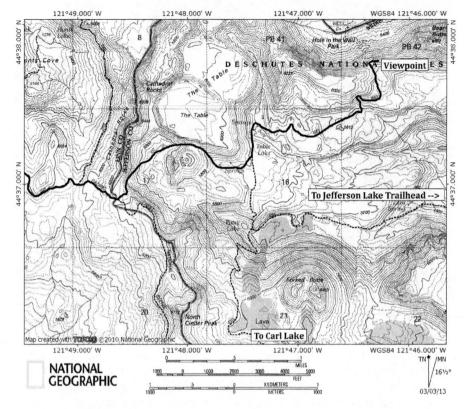

Where to start? If you follow user trails on the northwest side of the lake, you will pass springs lined with pink monkeyflower and fields of lupine to Upper Table Lake. As hard as this may be to believe, Upper Table Lake is even more aquamarine than its larger neighbor to the south. Please be careful where you step around here, as this area is quite fragile. Of those who come to Table Lake, many do so with the goal of climbing up onto the Table, with its vast parklands. Others seek out hidden ponds and meadows off-trail to the south of Table Lake. Perhaps the best side trip of them all is the 3 mile (round trip) trek to a viewpoint west of Bear Butte. From Table Lake, follow the Cabot Lake Trail as it bears left away from the lake. Though rarely maintained, the trail is blazed and quite easy to follow. You will ascend gently through meadows and mountain hemlock forest until you reach the ridge above Table Lake. Here the trail turns a hard left and begins a short, stiff climb as it enters forest burned in the 2003 B+B Complex fire. You will soon crest the ridge, where you will find a sign that reads "VIEWPOINT". Turn right and climb the obvious knoll, where you are met with an absolutely astounding view. The rugged, sharp profile of Mount Jefferson fills the sky just three miles to your north while hundreds of feet below you sits the hidden valley known as Hole-in-the-Wall Park. Early in the morning you are certain to see wildlife down in the vast meadows of the park. There are no adjectives to adequately describe the emotions one feels here. Regardless of what you decide to do at Table Lake, you should plan on at least one full day at the lake to maximize the time you have to explore. Any trip less than 3 days will be ultimately unsatisfying.

On the return trip, remember that the connector trail is located in the second meadow past Table Lake, not the first. In this meadow, you will angle to the southwest following the faint but obvious trail. Once past this spot the connector trail is easier to follow than it was coming from the west, and will take you less time than it did on the approach. After making your way through the narrow valley south of the Table, climb steeply up the hanging meadows to the ridge crest again. Once on the ridge, continue to the PCT. If you lose the trail in fields of lupine after cresting the ridge, simply heading straight (southwest) will lead you to the PCT. From here, turn right (north) and switchback down to the junction with the Hunts Creek Trail. Turn left and hike 1.6 miles to the junction with the Lake of the Woods Trail. Turn left, hike 2.2 miles to the Bingham Ridge junction, where you turn right again. Descend 3.4 miles through the burned and then pristine forest to the trailhead and your car.

Other hiking options:
Table Lake from Jefferson Creek: The traditional approach to Table Lake arrives from the east via a loop of the Jefferson Lake and Sugar Pine Ridge Trails. There are two obvious disadvantages to this approach. First of all, it requires another full hour of driving from Portland. Second and worst of all, both the Jefferson Lake Trail and Sugar Pine Ridge Trails are extremely brushy and have not been maintained since the B+B Complex Fire in 2003. The Deschutes National Forest considers both trails "impassible" (in their words) and has decided to abandon them permanently. Nevertheless, people have been getting through to Table Lake with considerable effort on the Jefferson Lake Trail. The Sugar Pine Ridge Trail, on the other hand, is probably lost forever due to brush.

To find this trailhead, drive east from Salem the length of OR 22 to its junction with US 20. Drive over Santiam Pass and continue approximately 10 miles (or a total of 16 miles from the junction with OR 22) to the Metolius River Road. Turn left here and drive 2.7 miles to a fork. Take the "Campgrounds" option and fork to the right. Drive 10.3 miles to a bridge over the Metolius River at Lower Bridge campground. Continue over the bridge and up the hill, where you finally leave the pavement. When you reach a fork, turn right at a sign for the Jefferson Creek Trailhead. Continue following signs another 4 miles to the end of FR 1292. The road network has been realigned here recently, creating confusion if you own an older map of the area. Follow the signs and you will be fine. The last mile of FR 1292 features a wonderful view of Mount Jefferson rising above the brushy slopes burned in the 2003 fire. Tree lovers will be delighted to discover what is believed to be the nation's largest Rocky Mountain Douglas-fir tree just 0.1 mile from the Jefferson Lake Trailhead. Pass a junction with the abandoned Sugar Pine Ridge Trail and continue straight, fighting through brush for 9 miles to a junction with the Cabot Lake Trail near Patsy Lake. Turn right and hike just under a mile to Table Lake.

Best Hikes by Category

Not sure where to hike? These lists will help you make a decision.

Best Wildflower Hikes (normal peak):
1. Silver Star Mountain (*June – August*)
2. Wild Cheat / Triangulation Peak (*July*)
3. Jefferson Park via South Breitenbush (*August*)
4. Lookingglass Lake (*August*)
5. Mary's Peak (*June*)
6. Stacker Butte (*May*)
7. Bald Butte (*June*)

Best Waterfall Hikes:
1. White River Falls
2. Cave Falls
3. Henline Falls
4. Rock of Ages Ridge
5. Black Hole Falls

Best Old-Growth Forest Hikes:
1. Valley of the Giants
2. Wild Cheat Meadow
3. Quartz Creek
4. Elk Lake Creek
5. Fifteenmile Creek

Best Fall Foliage Hikes:
1. Boulder Lake Loop
2. Indian Racetrack / Red Mountain
3. Ruddy Hill
4. Flag Point / West Point
5. Newton Road Loop

Best Hikes for Rainy Days:
1. Black Hole Falls
2. Salmonberry River (both ends)
3. Henline Falls
4. Newton Road Loop
5. Dry Creek Falls via Herman Creek

Best Family Hikes:
1. Boulder Lake (just to lake)
2. Goat Marsh Lake (short version)
3. Henline Falls
4. Hawk Mountain
5. St. Johns Bridge Loop

About the author:

Matt Reeder discovered his love of the outdoors at a young age and spent much of his childhood hiking and camping in the mountains east of Salem. Although he moved to Illinois when he was in high school, Oregon's scenic beauty stayed with him, eventually prompting him to move back to Oregon at age 24. He has spent the past four years hiking, camping, researching and writing *Off the Beaten Trail*, his first hiking guide.

He lives in Portland, Oregon with his wife Wendy. When not out on the trail, Matt spends his time teaching French, volunteering for the Mazamas and obsessing about music. He can be identified on the trail by his St. Louis Cardinals hat, a sign of his great love for the 2011 World Series Champions.